THE
INDUSTRIAL
DEVELOPMENT
OF
POLAND

ROSA LUXEMBURG

THE INDUSTRIAL DEVELOPMENT OF POLAND

by Rosa Luxemburg

Translated from the German by
Tessa DeCarlo

With an Introduction by
Lyndon H. LaRouche, Jr.

Campaigner Publications, Inc.

COGITO ERGO SUM

New York

The Industrial Development of Poland was first published in Leipzig in 1898 under the title *Die Industrielle Entwicklung Polens.*

Campaigner Publications, Inc.
University Editions
231 West 29th Street
New York, N.Y. 10001
Editor-in-Chief: Nancy Spannaus
Editor: Kathy Stevens
Book Designer: Libby Moriarty

The cover: Polish sugar refinery, circa 1880.

Printed in the United States of America

CONTENTS

Publisher's Note

This publication of the English-language translation of Rosa Luxemburg's 1898 doctoral dissertation inaugurates a new series of octavo paperbound texts being issued under the *University Editions* trade-style. These titles are being grouped in two series. The present book is number one in one of these two, *Political Science Series.* The second group is the *Physical Sciences Series.*

The selection of titles for these series is based on a policy of issuing important, ground-breaking knowledge in those areas for which other textbook publishers have not yet established the appropriate combination of publishing commitments and specialist authority. As those topical areas may later be covered competently by other publishers, Campaigner Publications will move on to new areas of pioneering for important conceptions "whose time has come."

For example, the considerations used in selecting titles for the *Physical Sciences Series* include the following:

Recent experiment and observation, notably concerning high energy-density plasmas and related topics, point toward crucial experiments of the sort which will enable us to supersede Maxwellian physics in general, and also paradox-ridden appreciations of quantum relations in particular. These research developments arise in the motivating context of a global energy crisis and a potentially disastrous, on-going demobilization of the nation's university and other basic research and development capabilities. For spice, Soviet breakthroughs in this general area have potentialities as the basis for qualitatively new dimensions of global weapons systems.

This is an area for which Campaigner Publications has exceptional competence at its disposal. LaRouche and Parpart have shown in several locations, (1) why and how the theoretical-conceptual apparatus originally elaborated as a contribution to political economy has proven appropriate to guiding solutions to the main problems of both Maxwellian physics and the special expressions of those same problems both in the Einstein-Weyl program for general relativity and prevailing appreciations of quantum relationships. Levitt, Bardwell and others have elaborated the significance of this approach to the phenomena associated with "non-linear effects" in energy-dense plasmas. (2)

Those observations exemplify the kinds of criteria employed. The selected titles will be directed to informing the reader of important, groundbreaking aspects of current scientific work, will represent a topical area for which Campaigner Publications commands exceptional special competence, and will also represent a topic which would not be efficiently treated by other publishers at that time.

The same criteria apply to selection of titles for the *Political Science Series.*

Political science is currently seized by a devastating crisis.

---

1. Cf., Uwe Parpart, "The Concept of the Transfinite," *The Campaigner,* Vol. 9, Nos. 1-2, Jan.-Feb. 1976; Lyn Marcus, *Dialectical Economics,* D.C. Heath, Lexington, Mass., 1975; Lyndon H. LaRouche, Jr., "Italy Lectures: What Only Communists Know," *The Campaigner,* Vol. 8, No. 10, Dec. 1975.

2. Cf., Dr. Steven Bardwell, "Frontiers of Science: Plasma Physics," *FEF Newsletter,* Vol. 1, No. 6, June 1976, and "Frontiers of Plasma Physics II: The history of the Theory and Observation of Ordered Phenomenon in Magnetized Plasmas," *FEF Newsletter,* Vol II, No. 2, Sept. 1976; Dr. Morris Levitt, "Linearity and Entropy: Ludwig Boltzmann and the Second Law of Thermodynamics," *FEF Newsletter,* Vol. II, No. 2, Sept. 1976.

PUBLISHER'S NOTE

The upsetting problem is typified by the emerging pattern of factional realignments throughout most of the world. The alliances between the U.S. Labor Party and U.S. conservative groups around issues of the Carter campaign, which have offended the deeply rooted prejudices of numerous observers, are merely an internal U.S.A. reflection of realignments already developed to a more advanced form in Western Europe and elsewhere. To emphasize the most obvious overall implication of such developments: the prevailing, almost-axiomatic presumptions of political science concerning the gradations of political "right" to "left" have been irreparably discredited.

A new principled conception of the *primary* basis for political factional alignments and differentiations has surfaced under present conditions of an aggravated general monetary crisis. The primary division is clearly not between "right" and "left." The primary division is between, on the one side, those assorted forces sharing commitment to technological progress through industrial and agricultural expansion, and, on the other side, those who propose or tolerate neo-Malthusian and kindred rationalizations for a form of monetarists' austerity involving general deindustrialization. Consequently, the old forms of political science doctrines have lost the capability of providing even a credible description of the main issues in current affairs.

These developments include several crucial demonstrations of the alternative political science theory which the Labor Committee current had developed and applied during the preceding period. For related reasons, that political current has recently emerged as an intellectual force of major catalytic influence in global affairs. These circumstances uniquely qualify Campaigner Publications to supply some of the essential, ground-breaking texts thorugh which extant political science departments may be rescued from an otherwise probable intellectual bankruptcy.

Although the texts issued in this series are designed for use in graduate and advanced undergraduate classrooms, it is intended that their suitability for such uses will enhance their usefulness to a significant number of skilled workers and others off-campus, and will aid in establishing the kind of workers' educational movement which the U.S. Labor Party, in particular, is committed to fostering.

National Policy Implications

The Carter campaign's preponderant commitment to low rates of real capital formation, and even to deindustrialization of such regions as New England and the midwestern industrial belt, predetermines the emergence of a multi-partisan alliance dedicated at the very least to minimizing such irreparable damage to our national economy. The years immediately ahead will be characterized in part, therefore, by a fight to maintain the nation's skilled industrial labor force, to maintain as high rates of real industrial and agricultural capital formation as possible, and to defend and enhance the scientific research and development capabilities of our universities and other relevant institutions.

The *University Editions* series are intended to aid that effort. Just as Thomas Gresham and his allies in their time concentrated in part on developing cadres of artisans, scientists and other innovators in behalf of Tudor England's technologically oriented economic development, so an educational effort in that same spirit is urgent today.

Such achievements are not attained by a mere emphasis upon education per se. Gresham's justified contempt for sixteenth century Oxford and Cambridge universities is appropriate for reference on that point. Education inspires and qualifies the cadres of technological progress insofar as the experience of education is one of moving into the forefront of those pioneering accomplishments in knowledge and practice which have relatively the greatest universal importance for our species. Creative innovation has nothing in common with "preciosity" or the mere impulsive eccentricities of the parochialist or astrally oriented individualist.

The proper task of the educator is to electrify the student by exposing those frontiers of knowledge and application in which the greatest new achievements of universal importance can be uncovered. It is such goals, properly defined, which motivate the student to that kind of sustained and impassioned intellectual compulsion to work, through which, and only through which, the campus novice assimilates the knowledge and rigorous methods of intellectual work peculiar to the great creative, pioneering intellects. Thus situating himself or herself as a participating contributor to general human progress, the student acquires the special sort of intellectual excitement which is otherwise the joy of being part of the great on-going work of our species.

Luxemburg
and the Crisis
in Political Science

During the approximate half century preceding the autumn 1973 petroleum crisis, the fact of Rosa Luxemburg's fame and influence during the 1898-1921 interval had always provided the potential clue to an urgent, sweeping discrediting of the prevailing political science dogmas. The discrediting has now been accomplished by different means. The acceleration of the general monetary crisis' effects, following the 1973 crisis, has nullified the presumably axiomatic gradations of political "right" through "left" upon which the edifice of political science doctrines had been premised.

Under these recent, new circumstances, the same facts which formerly could have upset accepted political science dogmas have acquired an altered usefulness. The Luxemburg case has now become a means to aid scholars' salvage efforts among the ruins of the demolished old political science.

The indicated thesis is unfolded as follows.

It is a simple description of the relevant literature from the 1898-1921 period to report that, during the 1898-1919 interval of her life, and for approximately two years following her assassination, even Luxemburg's critics preponderantly conceded her relative preeminence among the political spokesmen and authoritative theoreticians of the international social-democracy. The point to be stressed is not that fame in itself, rather, her fame is a fact of singular collateral importance for assessing the socialist movement's (and others') response, then and later, to the theses advanced in her *Accumulation of Capital. (1)*

It has been demonstrated, in locations published earlier *(2),* that the central economic-theoretical and related political theses advanced in her *Accumulation of Capital* and related writings *(3)* have been proven devastatingly correct *(4)* relative to the alternative views of all her notable contemporary critics and competitors. *(5)* Once the simple fact of her 1898-1921 authority as an *economic theoretician* is taken into account, the past half century's economic-theoretical disorientation of the socialist organizations can not be excused by the suggestion that her correct solutions to the problem of imperialist economy were in any sense the overlooked contributions of some obscure or dubious specialist.

Not only did her critics refuse to directly answer any of her principal systematic arguments and evidence then or later. To their greater discredit, the course of developments, from the onset of World War I through the rise of Nazism and World War II, precisely corresponded to Luxemburg's "model," and refuted the alternative "models" recommended by all of her various critics and competitors. Taking into account her economic-theoretical authority during the 1898-1921 interval, the behavior of the socialist movement on this matter must be described fairly

---

1 English translation, Schwarzchild, Monthly Review Press, New York, 1951.

2 Lyndon LaRouche (Lyn Marcus), *Dialectical Economics,* Lexington, Mass. 1975, Chapter 1; Lyn Marcus, "In Defense of Rosa Luxemburg," *The Campaigner* Vol. 6, No. 2, Spring 1973; in Rosa Luxemburg, *Anti-Kritik,* DeCarlo, et al., transl. *The Campaigner,* Vol. 5, No. 1, Jan.-Feb., and No. 3, Summer, 1972, "Preface."

3 *Anti-Kritik, Introduction to National Economy.*

4 Cf., Isaac Deutscher, *The Unfinished Revolution,* Oxford University Press, 1967. He credits her as vindicated "with a vengeance."

5 Cf., N.2, *supra.*

as permeated by *hysterical* irrationality, irrationality respecting an economic-theoretical issue of the type most vital to that movement's very existence.

Such hysteria reminds us that some persons, when ill, will flee into fabulously convoluted rationalizations, to justify following almost any advice but that of a qualified physician. Confronted with the fact of such behavior, only a sleepy-minded incompetent — or fellow-hysteric — could avoid the conclusion that the performance has been governed by some sensed need to conceal an awesome actual or imagined truth respecting the performer. So, the immediate facts of the Luxemburg case direct inquiry to such awesome truths concerning the old social-democracy, and thence to discovering the pervasive bankruptcy of the old political science doctrines in general.

The cited hysteria proves to involve two distinct but tactically interconnected causes: the evasions of those opponents whose philosophical world-outlook could not inhabit the same lawfully ordered universe as Luxemburg's, and the somewhat different but related hostilities of those social-democratic and other trimmers who were enraged that Luxemburg should again *(6)* undertake to spoil their policy of keeping one philosophical-political foot in each of two irreconcilable universes.

The context for that interplay is the characteristic paradox of the social-democracy and emerging Communist factions: the self-styled socialist movement has always been composed predominantly of two antagonistic philosophical currents, each less compatible with the other than with (at least potentially) some significant component of factional tendencies within the capitalist political camp.

Luxemburg's work was directed toward the kernel of this problem, like a triggering impulse directed toward an implanted explosive charge. If the factional issues involved in the Luxemburg case had not been suppressed with aid of the diversionary frauds of her combined opponents, the ensuing debate would have blown apart the principal socialist factions as they were then constituted. Such results would have affected the emerging

---

6   As in her earlier prompting of the factional attack against E. Bernstein, which she imposed upon a reluctant Wilhelm Liebknecht, Karl Kautsky and August Bebel, threatening them with an international scandal if they failed to take up the cudgels.

Communist International only less devastatingly than the old social-democracy.

The immediate cause for the philosophical dualism of the socialist movement is that nineteenth century capitalism itself was characterized primarily by a parallel dualism, its own set of analogous fundamental internal differences in embedded philosophical outlooks. On the one side, the capitalist currents emergent from the Renaissance and Enlightenment upsurges converged upon the primary generative principle of a commitment to realizing technological and cultural progress through industrial expansion and correlated agreeable new forms of agricultural development. At the same time, as has been emphasized in locations published earlier (7) , the English Restoration, the Hannoverians' Scottish highlands policies, and the emerging mercantilist-aristocratic colonial policies of England from the mid-1700s onward represented the growing relative hegemony of a policy which was preponderantly anti-industrialist in implications.

This latter policy, centered sociologically in the mercantilist colonialism of the British East India Company, allied to the rural imbecility of the gentry, tolerated *some* technological development, of course. It tolerated technological progress insofar as industrial development appeared to be a subordinated contributing means to the primary objective of augmenting rents and other mercantilist forms of *nominal* wealth.

Such underlying divisions in tendency within the ruling capitalist strata were directly reflected in the division of the socialist movement into what Marx and Engels chose to describe as the opposition of *scientific* versus *utopian* socialism. *(8)* The former paralleled and extended the capitalist industrialist outlook, of solving society's problems through technologically oriented expansion of total and per capita output. The latter paralleled the Benthamite and Malthusian outlooks and policies of the British East India Company and the Rothschilds, in emphasizing a struggle over "re-distribution" of an at least

---

7 Cf., *draft Constitution of the U.S. Labor Party*, New York, Dec., 1976, Sec. 1, *passim*.

8 N.B. Karl Marx, *1844 Manuscripts*, *The Poverty of Philosophy*, "Critique of the Gotha Programme," and also Marx and F. Engels, *The Holy Family* (*passim*), *The German Ideology* (*passim*), and F. Engels "Socialism, Utopian and Scientific."

relatively fixed scale of production under circumstances of relatively fixed productive technology.

Consequently, the crisis in political science implicitly triggered by the Luxemburg case could not have been contained within the socialist movement. The ruling currents of modern political science dogma, as typified in part by the U.S. "revisionist" historiography emerging following World War I, are premised on a commitment to deny the existence of the primary conflict permeating the past approximate eight centuries of European culture. If Luxemburg's *Accumulation* thesis is focussed appropriately upon the debate among the Allies concerning the German war-reparations feature of the Versailles Treaty, one begins to see directly how the implications of Luxemburg's case for the socialist movement must have spilled over to the same degree of devastating effect for political science doctrines in general.

To summarize the effect of the exposure of such bankruptcy of the old political science: world politics during the recent centuries to date is not properly characterized by a relatively linear gradation among feudal, capitalist and socialist factions. Rather, both the capitalist and socialist factions have each been divided in underlying fundamental tendencies of self-interested policy by a basic conflict between the "Idea of Progress" and what we today identify as neo-Malthusian doctrines of "cultural relativism."

It must be conceded, and even emphasized in this particular connection, that illusions or outright delusions in the minds of individuals and institutionalized forces may temporarily cause persons to act in behalf of such illusions. To this extent, a political doctrine based on empiricist acceptance of such illusions, illusions ranked analytically according to their apparent hegemonies, may appear for a while to afford reliable description and even predictive authority for actual social processes. It is principally for such reasons that some absurd political doctrines may secure for a time the reputation and influence of prevailing authority. Nonetheless, widespread belief in an illusion does not make it less an illusion. The discrepancy between a misdirected social practice based on illusion and the ignored reality does not vanish merely because "everyone" for a while prefers to mistake the illusion for reality. Rather, the cumulative discrepancy between underlying real processes and illusion-guided general practice is augmented to the point of an imminent, irrepressible crisis, at which point the institutions embodying the illusions must themselves be exploded.

It would have been better to dispense with such illusions earlier, by rational means, rather than postponing the matter until the explosion of the otherwise inevitable social crises. It would have been far better for mankind to have dispensed with the old illusions — the old political science dogmas — rationally, in the way in which the case of Luxemburg portended. Mankind did not; hence, the truth has lately asserted its existence through an irrepressible monetary crisis bordering upon the sharply increased probability of a global thermonuclear holocaust. While we yet survive, despite the manifest predominating stupidity on this question to date, it is not yet too late to learn what we should have learned earlier: that, during the immediately perilous future, we do not repeat the follies of stubborn blind faith in prevailing illusions.

In the remainder of this introduction, we shall summarize the direct connection between the Luxemburg case and the causes for the bankruptcy of the old political science doctrines. To this purpose, we first elaborate two main points somewhat separately from one another, and then show how these two are properly brought together to accomplish the relevant demonstrations.

The Two Points Identified

The *first* of these two phasal points, the Luxemburg case situated in the cited terms of historical reference, is developed with the aid of her 1898 doctoral dissertation, published here in its English-language edition.

The dissertation, because it is characterized to an extraordinary degree of maturity by the identical method and criteria more comprehensively developed in the *Accumulation of Capital* enables us to pin down the timing and circumstances of the development of her outlook with certainty. So demonstrating the philosophical-methodological consistency of her outlook from approximately the outset of her career, we are equipped to analyze her behavior and disputes within the international social-democracy from that standpoint.

This procedure by which this evidence is applied has the advantage of corresponding in effect to a "crucial experiment." It forces to the surface those underlying conflicts for which the nominal issues of factional disputes within the social-democracy were symptom and disguise. It leads to a singular demonstration of our stated hypothesis concerning that social-democracy. This identifies a positive proof, as distinguished from the inductive-statistical or kindred types of circumstantial, null-hypothesis-type demonstration. Accordingly, as we stated, it satisfies the conditions of a "crucial experiment." The importance of this is that such procedures are the proper means by which positive proof of a general principle (e.g., general law) is obtained for any field of inquiry.

This observation establishes the preconditions for connecting the Luxemburg case to the *second* phasal point: the already-cited fact that, up to the present, the socialist movement so-called has been torn by underlying conflicts between two principal included currents, currents so opposed in primary characteristics of practical philosophical world-outlook that their incompatibility is comparable to that between the primary characteristics of two universes constituted of mutually exclusive geometries. For convenience, these may be differentiated, as we have noted above, in terms of the conflict between *scientific* and *utopian* socialist currents.

Since we must aim to situate the Luxemburg case within the historical context in which it developed, we reverse the order, to begin here with the second of the two points.

The Form of the Conflict

The *scientific* current has been a direct continuation into the socialist movement of the humanist philosophical outlook of the European Renaissance and capitalist Enlightenment. To those socialists, as to the gigantic Arab Renaissance intellect known to Europeans as Avicenna, and to Avicenna's European successors — Roger Bacon, Marsilio Ficino, Pico della Mirandola, Rene Descartes, Benedict Spinoza, et al. — the *voluntary* element of human creative innovations has been the *primary* quality of human existence, and also the uniquely appropriate basis for determination of individual practice and general social policy.

That humanist notion of human *freedom* has nothing in common with anarchism, but denounces arbitrary individual wilfulness (*heteronomy*) as the essential quality of human wickedness. Freedom — or, for emphasis, *lawful* freedom — has been limited by humanist conception to that ongoing specific development of voluntary innovation which was *demonstrably appropriate* to lawful universal orderings of natural causal relations. Beginning approximately with Thomas Gresham, the adopted (as accessible) form of crucial test of human knowledge, of what innovative impulses were or were not appropriate, has been technological progress as manifest for capitalist development by industrialized progress in man's per capita mental and productive power over the material universe.

Accordingly, the *scientific,* or Marxist socialist current proceeded from an original policy commitment to *capitalist* forms of extended reproduction. Marx's later socialist perspectives, like his four-volume *Capital,* always retained the adduced capitalist form of extended reproduction as the foundation to be superseded. During the 1843-1871 period, Marx's capitalist and socialist revolutionary impulses were concurrent and interdependent, premised upon a common set of axiomatic commitments.

The process leading into the 1848 revolution was for Marx (among others) a fight for industrial-*capitalist* economic and political (republican) forms against the brutish obscenities of the Holy Alliance. This perspective for the establishment of a German national republic remained dominant in Marx's practical political commitments up to the Franco-Prussian war's mid-point. The capitalist side of Marx's political perspectives is underlined by such writings as those devoted to Palmerston and Russell, his *Herr Vogt, (9)* and otherwise the policies of Marx, Engels and Joseph Weydemeyer bearing upon the U.S. Civil War.

Marx's socialist perspectives originated in his perception of

---

9 His *Secret Diplomatic History,* his papers on Palmerston and Russell in several forms during the 1850s and first half of the 1860s, his *18th Brumaire, Civil War in France,* and *Herr Vogt* show that Marx was very close to the truth concerning the Pitt-Palmerston-Canning-Russell-Rothschild operations of the first three-quarters of the 19th century. His (and Weydemeyer's) role concerning the Republican Party during the 1850s and 1860s, defending the U.S. against the British colonialists sponsoring and using the Confederacy in an effort to "balkanize" the United States is a crucial feature of any study of Marx's political method and outlook.

those conflicts within capitalist strata which prevented such strata from consistently realizing the industrialist-republican perspective. The "parliamentary cretinism" exhibited by the German and other capitalist republicans during the onset and course of the 1848 revolution was for him a typification of those characteristic internal weaknesses of the capitalist strata which demanded the handing-over of political leadership to a new principal force, a politically unified working class to be constituted as a virtual *class-for-itself*.

The included relevance of such facts is the already-stated point that Karl Marx was for most of his adult life *simultaneously* a capitalist revolutionary and a socialist revolutionary. Or, to state the same point in terms better suited to analysis, *as a developing socialist revolutionary* Marx was a *practicing* capitalist revolutionary for most of that life. The relationship between those ironical, but not paradoxical commitments originates in a common set of primary policy principles.

The subsumed principal policy criteria included: (a) the optimal maximization of the social surplus produced by the *society as a whole;* (b) the realization of that surplus as the *mediation* (*not* the end) of more technologically advanced forms of industrial and agricultural production on an enlarged scale, (c) with increasing domination of the *world as a whole* by such successive technological and productive advancements. These criteria were conditional *for Marx* upon (d) per capita increases in output as embodying a *secular associated tendency for* increases in the material quality of household consumption and of other preconditions for a culturally advancing labor force *as a whole.*

Such specific forms of per capita increases in output, uniquely dependent upon associated successive "layers" of technological advancements, are identified as a unique solution to the otherwise paradoxical combined requirement of simultaneously increasing social surplus rates and satisfying rising material consumption and leisure requirements for the *world as a whole.* In all aspects of Marx's elaboration of such conceptions, the *whole* was taken to be a *primary,* self-subsisting existence; this was in opposition to the reductionist outlooks, which treat whole societies as derived aggregations of component, "primary" elements.

For reasons related to this point, Marx and Engels' adoption of the term *utopian* for the opposing current has unfortunate, potentially misleading included implications. The term was admittedly strongly recommended by the performance of the so-called utopian socialists themselves; Cabet, Proudhon, Weitling, et al., the names associated with the origins of such currents, were pathetic parodies of Sir Thomas More. They purported to spin entire, "perfected" societies from the gland of their own and their dupes' common neurotic prejudices. They were characterized collectively by the manifest desire *to be seen as utopians.* They were rightly, satirically to be termed "utopians" to the same effect that the infantry company's archetypical "sad sack" might acquire the barracks-name of "colonel" or "general." Yet, at the same time, in philosophical outlook and method, Proudhon, et al. embodied everything for which such Renaissance utopians as Marsilio Ficino had profound and justifiable contempt. *(10)*

The relevance of our stipulation here is underlined by the fact that the European Avicenneans from Roger Bacon, through Ficino, into Descartes, and Spinoza were the proper forerunners of Hegel and Marx.

Ficino's Renaissance utopianism was premised upon a demonstration of the primary quality of those voluntary innovations *in conformity with* the universal ordering of nature. Since Ficino defined the universal ordering of nature as effectively pre-ordained, for him and for kindred Renaissance utopians the voluntary process of human *self-perfection* must converge upon the asymptote of exact correspondence between the moments of the human will and the pre-ordained laws. *(11)*

The later shift in the perspective of humanism was the leading philosophical accomplishment of the European Enlightenment, representing a dialectical method which was the crucial epistemological distinction between the Renaissance and the Enlightenment. Beginning, most notably, with René Descartes, and first explicitly argued to this effect by B. Spinoza,

---

10   Marsilio Ficino, *Five Questions Concerning the Mind.* Cf., Dr. S. Pepper, "Art and NeoPlatonism in the Renaissance," *The Campaigner*, Vol. 10, Nos. 1-2, Jan. 1977. Also, LaRouche "Italy Lectures: What Only Communists Know," *The Campaigner*, Vol. 8, No. 10, Dec. 1975.

11   *ibid.*

the notion of a pre-ordained fixed goal was superseded — without otherwise rejecting any of the essential humanist principles of Ficino, et al. Descartes' rudimentary notion of a space-time-matter continuum, and related contributions of Spinoza, anticipated embryonically the notion of a *Riemannian transfinite* solution to the "unified field" problem. (As that notion has been shown to be partly explicit and otherwise implicit in the retrospective application of the leading contributions of Georg Cantor to Riemann's work. *(12)*) For Spinoza, *perfection* was not a succession of isolable individual acts of discovery, but an existent, continuous, determining ordering-principle, whose self-elaboration was its own substance and end.

To illustrate the crucial conception: this is the same as saying for physics that the laws of the universe are not fixed, but represent a nested succession of sets of coherent universal laws, each set of which might *momentarily appear as if it were fixed.* This is the result which appears if we apply the notion of a *Riemannian transfinite* to obtain a coherent connection between existing continuous laws of the universe and the otherwise para-doxical singularities lawfully situated in that same universe. *(13)* Each set of momentary universal laws then becomes logically an included predicate, sub-set, of a continuous (negentropic) unifying principle, a principle which subsumes and determines the ordered succession of negentropically-order-ed evolutions of universal laws. This process can have no beginning and no end. The subsuming process itself must be comprehended as an *existent* relative transfinite (not a mere mental construct) for the predicated sets of universal laws it subsumes. It must otherwise, as such a transfinite, conform to the notion of an *existent self-subsisting positive principle*, as successively elaborated for epistemology by Spinoza, Hegel, Feuerbach, and Marx.

It happens to be the present case, that such a conception of physics is at the moment only better than an hypothesis,

---

12   Uwe Parpart, "The Concept of the Transfinite," *The Campaigner*, Vol. 9, Nos. 1-2, Jan.-Feb. 1976.

13   LaRouche, "Rockefeller's Fascism With A Democratic Face," Sec. 2, *The Campaigner*, Vol. 8, Nos. 1-2, Nov.-Dec., 1974; see also the Introduction to "The Concept of the Transfinite" by Parpart, *op. cit.*

advantaged by some powerful crucial-experimental demonstrations in the domain of negentropic "nonlinear effects." Although it has been shown by such "crucial experiments" to be qualitatively superior to the formerly hegemonic but paradoxical Maxwellian physics, it must be termed an hypothesis out of respect for the fact that a coherent elaboration of the indicated theoretical apparatus has yet to be accomplished.

That present circumstance of physics is no defect in the point previously made. The case for such a "physics" has already been conclusively made for the universal ordering of human existence. Some brief comment upon that point is required at this juncture.

The crucial fact of human species existence is that without a correlated alteration of the human genetic nature, the technology and associated cultural forms developed by our species have enabled us to advance from the mode of existence and ecological population-potential of a gifted baboon to a population approaching four billion today. Furthermore, provided controlled thermonuclear reactions are rapidly developed as a primary energy source, with existing industrial and agricultural technology at approximately their present level of advancement, the earth could sustain a population of tens of billions of persons at a higher modal level of household existence than presently prevails among less than four billion. The sole cause for this absolute distinction between the human species and lower beasts is man's manifest potential for creative innovation, a potential creativity which has thus cumulatively demonstrated itself to be in masterful conformity with underlying primary laws of the universe.

Consequently, this negentropic essential principle of human existence, behavior, *and of individual human nature*, is manifest in the study of society in such a way that no competent general conclusions or science of human behavior could be premised upon anything but that "Avicennean" dialectical notion. A comparison of *Dialectical Economics* and related writings *(14)*, embody that principle as the axiomatic premise of economic processes' analysis, with the way in which the current general monetary crisis has evolved, exemplifies the crucial demonstra-

---

14   Cf., N. 12, 13.

tions of the proven unique authority of such principles for the domain of the social sciences.

The specific relevant difficulty of mathematical physics heretofore is that its practical commitments have been broadly delimited to exploring those aspects of natural phenomena and human intervention in nature which correspond to the special cases for which apparent entropy characterized such processes. Sensitive physicists and others long have been conscious of devastating paradoxes in such a prevailing approach, but until recently physics in general has been unable to foresee any effective well-defined approach to remedy such paradoxes, nor has it until recently discovered any urgent practical reason which obliged it to embark upon such revolutionary enterprises. Hence, the physicist in general has avoided the problems of formulating a negentropic physics abstractly or defining crucial experiments in behalf of hypotheses subsumed by such an abstract inquiry.

Recently, a change in the situation of physics has begun. In retrospect, even on the basis of accomplishments to date, we can better appreciate the circumstantial impediments existing in the past to such an enterprise.

Soviet experiments with coherent beams aimed at the ionosphere and correlated evidence of negentropic "nonlinear effects" structures in energy-dense plasmas (the ionosphere is an energy-dense plasma in the sense that the field energy content is greater than the thermal energy content) on the surface of the earth, in the search for energy-breakeven in controlled thermonuclear reactions, have forced a recent abrupt shift of thinking among leading currents of the international physics community. In general, the sort of negentropic effects (as primary phenomena) to which we have referred are manifest prominently only in energy-dense plasmas and related cases, whereas relatively low-energy-density phenomena can be predictively assessed in terms of axiomatic notions of entropy as primary. (This distinction has a direct relevance for the application of the sort of Riemannian geometries we have pointed toward.)

Sociologically, the breakthrough from an entropic toward a negentropic physics correlates with our present historic impulse to master energy-dense phenomena, *historic* because this correlates with the need to increase the energy-density of human productive and household existence.

Consequently, it is no sign of defect in the notion of an existent self-subsisting positive principle as primary, that what presently passes for ordinary consciousness may often find such notions alien and otherwise disagreeable. Such objections merely indicate some of the important contributing reasons most professed Marxists have been mentally incompetent to comprehend fully and directly Marx's own most essential notions and world-outlook. In tomorrow's world — on condition that we survive the present global crisis — such notions will have become the commonplaces of physical science, and will have drifted into appropriate degrees of comprehensibility among laymen. Meanwhile, if such notions may remain difficult by reputation insofar as they are applied to physics qua physics, they are fully demonstrated for the characteristically negentropic processes of human development, and thus immediately thoroughly grounded in practice and more or less fully comprehensible with respect to that frame of reference of inquiry.

Although this post-Enlightenment line of conceptual development separates the dialectical currents of scientific socialism from the Renaissance utopianism of Ficino, et al., in all other essential respects the nineteenth century utopian socialists so-called are the common, irreconcilable enemies of both Ficino and the scientific socialists.

In the same vein, Marxian socialism shares with Christian humanism the subsumed principle that the human individual as a human personality is, firstly, a universally determined individual existence (not a self-evidently individual existence qua individual existence), and secondly, that the essence of the individual human existence is its proper obligation to bring its consciousness and practice into conformity with a purpose properly universal to the human species. The individual act must be positive in its ultimate practical implications for human development *as a whole*...hence, *universality*. In Hegelian language, the individual is properly governed in the development of his consciousness and in his practical behavior by the determination to act knowledgeably as a *world-historical personality*.

It is by virtue of their hostility to this latter, subsumed point of agreement between Marxists and Christian humanists that the utopians essentially differentiated themselves from all humanism.

In parody of Rousseau's foolish "social contract" and so forth, the utopian socialists proceeded from the embedded axiomatic presumption that the human individual was essentially a "talking animal" whose primary nature was that of a self-evidently individual existence governed by "individual greed." Although particular utopian currents may have at one moment or another attached themselves to isolated parts of the universalizing moral sentiments of their society, this was more of an adaptation than an expression of their essential outlook. To the extent they made themselves more perfectly consistent with their essential outlook, in the direction suggested by Max Stirner and others, (15) they rejected any universal humanistic determination of individual human nature, and were at best indifferent to any universal purpose but that of discovering some agreeable accomodation among individual greeds.

In all of the hereditary implications of that axiomatic assumption of Stirner, et al., the scientific and utopian socialists belonged absolutely to different universes. The essential, formal-epistemological opposition between the two currents was the opposition of the standpoint of humanist universality to that of such vulgar philosophical reductionisms as behaviorism and "cultural relativism."

In summary of the point: the so-called utopians defined all problems of social policy from the embedded axiomatic premise of "individual greed." For them, society was defined as a mere aggregation of individual greedinesses. For them, socialism could be nothing but this or that proposed *re-distribution* of whatever each utopian cult presented as its laundry-list of notable goodies for such reallocations. Fabian ILPer George Orwell's *Animal Farm*, his *1984* and the Orwellian nightmare, *Clockwork Orange*, are properly included among the predicated versions of the utopian-socialist schematizings.

Just as they otherwise adapted themselves to moral sentiments prevailing among their would-be constituencies, some

---

15 Cf., *The German Ideology* on Stirner and his "The Ego and its Own." Police provocateur, Rothschild agent, and all-around scoundrel Bakunin professed himself to have synthesized Proudhon and Stirner to create his own doctrine of anarchism.

utopian and successor currents have, at one time or another, associated themselves with demands for technological progress. In such instances, it is demonstrable that such support for technological progress have never reflected a primary concern with human development as a universality. In the overt or shamefaced expressions of utopian traditions, the occasional tract dedicated to the theme "What will life be like under socialism?" exposed the mind of the utopian. Insofar as technology in particular is concerned, such professed socialists would make a "workers paradise" of either the present-day society "without certain of its defects," or imagine some work-free pastoral idyll characterized by a life organized around creek-fishing and sundry purposeless hobbies. For them, progress has never been valued as better than an optional, secondary demand to be included or omitted from the utopian laundry-list of goodies for redistribution.

As a philosophical outlook, as expressed by the common underlying features of the overall arguments and practice of the utopians and their successors, the utopian tradition has been associated with "models" for which the specification of "zero growth" and "cultural relativism" could be included without significant alteration of the resulting judgments.

Utopian socialism is not limited to the early nineteenth century Proudhonists and such, or merely the cults which purport to directly imitate original nineteenth century utopian forms. Anarchism and anarchosyndicalism today are utopianism degenerated into the forms convergent upon philosophical fascism. "Third Campism," a variant of anarchosyndicalism, is another explicit derivative from Proudhon, Stirner, et al. Otherwise, the gist of the utopian's reductionist outlook became the dominant feature of the international social-democracy from the founding of the German Social-Democracy (SPD). This is exemplified by the circumstances and contents of Karl Marx's "Critique of the Gotha Programme." *(16)*

In the case of the SPD, the heteronomic "greed" of the party's fragmented constituency organizations and the trade unions (as heteronomic agencies) governed the social-demo-

---

16   The founding program of the German Social-Democracy, and hence the hegemonic document of the Socialist (second) International until at least the 1891 adoption of the "Erfurt Program."

cracy's practice and practical thought. As analysis of the dichotomized Erfurt Program attests *(17)* , the SPD did also profess nominal forms of universal, socialist objectives — which it more or less consistently relegated to the oratory of party conferences and other domains of the ineffable.

This conflict between the scientific and utopian socialist currents was the issue of Marx's "Critique of the Gotha Programme" and the issue of the 1898-1899 "revisionism debate." Eduard Bernstein, attaching himself overtly to Fabian circles immediately following the death of Friedrich Engels, became the most visible Fabian (British Foreign Office) agent of influence within the German Social-Democracy (paralleling Fabian agent Legien of the trade unions, Vollmar, left-covered British agent Alexander Helphand-Parvus, and secret British agent August Bebel). The importance of the "revisionism debate" was not Bernstein's technical standing in the SPD apparatus or the overall disgusting mediocrity and recurring outright dishonesty of his theses. The importance of the debate was the fact that Bernstein's Fabianism found extensive echoes within the ranks and apparatus of the SPD more generally, a broad tendency for agreement with the meliorist, redistributionist syncretizings of Sidney Webb, George Bernard Shaw, and (later) Bertrand Russell.

Luxemburg, almost alone, represented the standpoint of scientific socialism in that debate — as subsequent developments clarified. Bernstein and his allies represented Fabian utopianism, while the center — including Bebel, Kautsky, et al. — sought to maintain the unity of the SPD by planting their feet in both the scientific and Fabian camps, opposing any "factional excesses" which might upset the precarious balance between the two social currents. Later, Bebel's center shifted over entirely to the utopian (meliorist) camp, in the aftermath of the 1905-1906 developments.

---

17   Gerry Rose, "The Social-Democracy's Roots," *The Campaigner*, Vol. 5, No. 2, March-April, 1972. Kautsky's draft for the 1891 ("Erfurt") SPD conference was proposed by Wilhelm Liebknecht, under pressure of Engels' threats to make a scandal over the SPD's suppression of Marx' letter attacking the Gotha Draft ("The Critique of the Gotha Programme"). Kautsky's draft contained two analytical elements: on the one hand, the "minimum program," the notion of a laundry-list of meliorist and related demands; on the other hand, the "maximum program," a mere edifying decoration, to be worshipped but not to be taken seriously for any practice but rhetorical flourishes on festive occasions.

The fight between scientific socialism and utopianism was also the fundamental issue of the 1913-1921 *Accumulation of Capital*.

Origins of the Conflict

The huge, accumulated war debt of England at the close of the Napoleonic wars was transformed into a kind of marriage-contract among the leading liberals, the British East India Company, and London financial powers soon dominated by the insurgent House of Rothschild. The common philosophical outlook unifying these forces found broad agreement among the rural gentry, a stratum whose conscience had never fully advanced beyond the zero-growth bestiality of the Norman Domesday Book. The hegemony of that cabal committed Great Britain to a colonialist-mercantilist policy of exporting enforced relative economic and cultural backwardness, and for home consumption (or, underconsumption) Malthusian forerunners of the monetarist austerity policies of Hjalmar Schacht and Schacht's bathetic imitator, Milton Friedman.

The most notable expression of such British domination of the continent for the development of the socialist movement was Britain's imposition of the bestial Holy Alliance under the mediating supervision of Rothschild puppet Metternich.

The Holy Alliance, as a policy, was a direct outgrowth of British rage against the American Revolution, rage against the French Revolution, and enraged reaction against the aborted echoes of the American Revolution in turn-of-the-century England itself. The British policy during the French Revolution, the Napoleonic wars and afterward was immediately to reduce France itself to relatively a second-rate economic and military power, and, more broadly, to prevent the influence of the French Revolution from leading to the establishment of strong, independent capitalist republics among other continental nationalities.

In fact, as in the consciousness of most of the leading intellects of that period, the early nineteenth century political movements of continental Europe were a continuation of the French Revolution and its culture throughout France, Germany, Italy and so forth. These struggles took the characteristic form of pro-capitalist nationalist struggles against (ultimately) the

British oppressor and, more emphatically, the British Foreign Office's Czarist "agent of influence." Immediately, this took the form of a struggle for overthrow of the Holy Alliance and of the bucolic aristocratic obscenities which the Metternichean order perpetuated throughout the localities of Europe.

The frontier for development of that new form of the French Revolution was Germany, the Rhine and its principal tributaries.

Germany was politically divided after 1815 into two leading parts. In those areas which had thus benefited from French occupation, notably the Rhineland regions, the rudiments of capitalist industrial development had sprung up *along the main artery of cheap inland freight*, the Rhine. To the east lay the growing power of Prussia. The outcome of the contention between these two contending leading forces within Germany largely determined the subsequent course of European history and the subsumed history of the socialist movement.

As a Germany battered by the Thirty Years War resumed population growth, the region which became Prussia of the late seventeenth and eighteenth centuries developed as a band of German agricultural development, a frontier migration of settlers from all parts of Germany and Switzerland, brought by the Prussian princes to build up their occupation and development of domains exacted from variously displaced and conquered slavic populations. Prussia's development thus exploited the collapse of Polish urban culture, which collapse had occurred during the period of general European economic and cultural decline under the Hapsburg rule of the sixteenth and early seventeenth centuries. With the economic collapse of the previously developing slavic urban culture and the weakening of the Hapsburg power throughout the Empire, the Prussian house emerged as a revitalized "marcher lord" force on the intersection between the German and slavic populations in the north.

It was for this combination of reasons that the relatively backward Prussian "marcher lord" frontier settlements became the ironic economic basis in cabbages and such for a major military power.

Such phenomena had been characteristic of the feudal and Renaissance periods. Feudal European powers had evolved a policy of settling rambunctious feudal military settlements along borders. Such frontier settlements, habituated to the conquest and other occasions of bloody affray with the populations they were appointed to contain, naturally produced the phenomenon of the "marcher lord," the bumptious, hardened military force which frequently revolted against its nominal sovereign. The King of France's settlement of the Normans as such a marcher-lord force in the north of France is exemplary of the principle. Prussia of the eighteenth and early nineteenth century was in those particular respects such a throwback, emergent after the temporary relative collapse of central European culture during the Hapsburg period.

The gist of the decisive conflict between the Rhineland and Prussia during the early nineteenth century can be appropriately summarized: either the superior culture of the Rhineland would develop a military force able to bring Prussia under its domination, or the military force of Prussia would assimilate the Rhineland. The outcome would more or less inevitably be determined by the balance of the uneasy alliance of Britain and Prussia against France and the Rhineland.

Indeed, that tradition persisted into the Rhineland of the 1920s, during which time a Rhinelander movement, with which later West German Chancellor Konrad Adenauer was then associated, weakly proposed an independent Rhineland state under de facto French protection, free of Prussian rule. The traditions of that Rhinelander-Prussia conflict are sometimes echoed in a curious way as an accent feature of the post-war politics of divided Germany. The included failures of the 1848 revolution foretold the result, and the circumstances of the Franco-Prussian war settled the matter for the ensuing period.

This case should not be grotesquely simplified to the false and silly presumption that Prussia was homogeneously opposed to industrial development. It soon became an advocate and sponsor of "Colbertian" industrial development, without its unwanted republican correlatives. Although the Hohenzollern house had a sometimes fetishistic attachment to its cabbage-junker officer corps, the Hohenzollern policy had remained organically what it had been since the recruitment of Swiss and German-speaking colonists to the "marcher lord" region. In this respect, Hegel's description of the Prussian State was well-informed if otherwise epistemologically superficial.

The Hohenzollerns were "bonapartist" monarchs, ruling

through a careful balancing and counter-balancing of contending social forces, principally expressed as a division between the civil and military bureaucracies and characterized by the primacy afforded to the military-aristocratic ranks. The plebeians were kept from rising into the military establishment, and the military-aristocratic strata discouraged from "degrading" themselves in plebeian occupations. The industrial development of Germany under the anti-republican Hohenzollerns, including the cases of Silesia and Saxony, exhibits the workings of the "marcher lord" mentality.

The notable difference was that the Rhinelander republicans aspired to make a German "French Revolution," whereas the Prussian state wished only to assimilate the technological accomplishments of French culture in the anti-republican form specifically advantageous to Prussianism.

The case of G.W.F. Hegel properly exemplifies this process within nineteenth century Germany.

Hegel was, during the onset of his adult life, temporarily an admirer of Napoleon Bonaparte. The world-historical figure of reference for the writing of Hegel's *Phenomenology* was Napoleon. As German nationalism rose against the continued Napoleonic political occupation and taxation, Hegel transferred his youthful admiration for the flesh-and-blood Napoleon to the grey abstraction of the Prussian monarchy. This turn, carried to its logical outcome in Hegel's *Philosophy of Right*, separated Hegel from his former followers and admirers among the republican "Hegelian left." From the Napoleonic period of German culture, the cases of Hegel's contemporaries, Beethoven and Goethe, are notable for comparison on this point, with Beethoven's embedded philosophical outlook, like that of Robert Schumann and the *pre-1848* Feuerbachian, Richard Wagner, placing Beethoven on Hegel's political left and Goethe somewhat to Hegel's political right.

It was, in sum of this point, two divergent outgrowths of the influence of the French Revolution which consciously shaped all of the insurgent political movements on the European continent during the first portion of the nineteenth century, for which revolutionary Rhinelanders and their allies, such as Marx, Schumann and (by adopted preference) Heinrich Heine, typified the French current; those allied with Prussia, and to that degree ultimately with Britain, the policy of following only a constrained, anti-republican version of the French Revolution's influence.

Since the pro-capitalist, republican nationalists formed their thoughts against the backdrop of the French Revolution, they extended conceptions so determined into all principal features of their outlook. In themselves, the German republicans centered along the Rhine were successors of Kant, Fichte and Hegel, thus in those various ways embodiments of the Enlightenment. Moreover, they rightly considered themselves become superior to France in philosophy and still inferior to France in political-economy and the physical sciences. Overall, they saw themselves imminently as the allies of a revolutionary France in common cause against the Holy Alliance.

They foresaw such a common, continental revolutionary upsurge as given substance by a rising of the sans-culottes under the leadership and direction of a political intelligentsia drawn principally from liberal republican strata. This preconception guided their approach to the proletarian strata and their interventions into ferment within such strata.

In this circumstance, the intellectual currents emanating from and through the mediation of various factions of the liberal intelligentsia determined the corresponding characteristic political currents of those emerging socialist currents influencing the artisan and working-class layers. Since European capitalist development and culture was itself an ongoing conflict between insurgent pro-industrialist and relatively hegemonic monetarist-aristocratic forces, the characteristic philosophical outlooks of each capitalist political current were reflected accordingly in whichever forms selectively proved most appropriate to the sociological composition of the fostered socialist currents.

In Germany, some endemic psychic disorders contributed to this process. Specifically, the pathetic romanticism typified by the awful poetry of Klopstock and the sentimental slop of the brothers Schlegel, the pseudo-impassioned banality of spirit otherwise celebrated by the institution of "Kitsch." In this pathetic German form of European romanticism the germs of utopian socialism found a reception. To the ultra-individualistic young would-be intellectual, acting out his infantile, oedipal individuality in convoluted forms of imagined and actual seductions, his infantile, oedipal existentialist acts of imagined, attempted and actual suicides — what were classes, or, indeed, the real world, for him? He must arbitrarily fashion a society agreeable to his heteronomic conceits. This miserable fellow found a satisfying momentary emotional drunkeness in steeping himself (in fact or fantasy) in the criminal impulsions of the brutalized lumpen strata. From such elements as himself and these lumpen cronies, from such a fantasy of a beggar's opera, the forerunners of Mark Rudd, et al. spun out images of the "ideal society," and formed the mayfly cults out of which the utopian socialist current as a whole emerged.

Karl Marx typified the currents of thought which attempted to discover the necessary causal correlation between the development of culture and the technological changes characteristic of capitalist industrial development. Marx's original concern was to effect the establishment of, in particular, a German capitalist republic, his continuing practical concern through and beyond the 1848 revolution. In that respect he was epistemologically and politically a left-Hegelian.

In the course of this work, Marx discovered the conception of the working-class forces potentially transformed into a political class-for-itself. His conception of the historic role of such an independent political class force had nothing in common with the beggar's-opera socialism of the utopians. It was not the brutalized, atomized individual worker assembled into a mob, not the utopian's beggar's-opera army of proletarians, but a collection of such persons lawfully transformed in the form of their common association and self-consciousness which was Marx's *class-for-itself.* (18)

Marx's appreciation of such a class-for-itself force always had two derived, interconnected practical points in view. Immediately, especially respecting the 1848 revolution, Marx located in the political class-for-itself *a combative quality* much to be desired in contrast to the "parliamentary cretinism" and kindred deplorable qualities exhibited by the liberals. The working class, becoming a political class-for-itself, was to Marx originally the proper instrument for establishing a German

---

18 Cf., Karl Marx, "Feuerbach" (*passim*) *The German Ideology, The Poverty of Philosophy, The Communist Manifesto,* for Marx's formulation of the working-class force's transformation from a fragmented class into a class as a whole.

republic committed to *capitalist forms of economic development*. Secondly, after the discovery that such a class-for-itself represented a consciously world-historical force for realizing the economic objectives of capitalist industrial development, the emergence of such an agency potentially dispensed with further need for capitalist *political* forms of (*heteronomic*) individual ownership of the principal means of production and distribution.

Hence, Marx's view developed into the following summary form. The *initial* function of the struggle to develop an atomized working class into a conscious class-for-itself was to force the furtherance of the capitalist revolution. At the point that the capitalist political forces failed to continue capitalist forms of economic development at some crucial juncture, the political class-for-itself must take over the capitalists' former such leading role. Having assumed political direction of the capitalist form of the productive forces as a conscious, centralized agency, the emergence of the class-for-itself superseded the need to continue that economic development through capitalist political forms: *socialism*.

As Marx emphasized in the *Communist Manifesto*, his conception of the class-for-itself coincided with those broad political upsurges in which masses of workers broke out of previously hegemonic forms of localized institutions and narrowly defined self-interests, to deploy themselves as a unifying force on behalf of programmatic commitments to general economic development and against reactionary political forms. In the course of what Rosa Luxemburg later analyzed as "political mass strike" upsurges, (19) the implicit philosophical world-outlook of working people was, at least temporarily, significantly transformed in the direction of a class-for-itself outlook. To the extent that such movements and impulses were manifest in the working-class proper or among intellectuals kindred to Marx himself, these features of social development provided a social basis for institutionalizing the Marxist, or scientific socialist current.

Directly opposite to Marx, the Proudhonists, and such a peripatetic Metternichean police-provocateur of the 1840s and 1850s as Bakunin, radiated what was appropriately termed the "petit-

---

19 *The Mass Strike...*, various English-language editions of the Integer translation.

bourgeois" philosophical outlook of the mercantilist capitalist faction, of the Benthamites, the Malthusians, of the House of Rothschild — for which Bakunin, later funded in part through Rothschild Russian agent Herzen, was directly a leading agent (late 1860s, 1870s). Fabianism, a direct creation and long-time political intelligence cover of the British Foreign Office and the Rothschild circles, and such syncretists' outgrowths of Fabianism as anarchosyndicalism and philosophical fascism, were other features of the utopian current's emergence as a direct result of the influence of the mercantilist-colonialist faction upon appropriate "radical" strata.

The Analytical Problem

The central formal error of the now-bankrupted doctrines of political science is reflected in the blunder of compiling data respecting capitalist society as if the ostensibly capitalist factions and manifest capitalist interest in major issues were (*post hoc ergo propter hoc*) homogeneously capitalist. This difficulty has not been entirely overlooked; unfortunately, the most commonplace inconsistencies acknowledged have been speciously resolved by resort to a pseudo-category, "semi-feudal." It has not been recognized that the dominant currents of nominal capitalist interest embody two fundamentally antagonistic currents. This is most forcefully demonstrated in the case of the blundering approach which adopts early nineteenth century England as approximating a "model" of "pure, competitive capitalism."

The associated, complicating problem in attempting to distinguish the opposing component currents within capitalist factions, is that the capitalist accumulation process includes both the impulse for technologically oriented industrial and agricultural development on a global scale, and also the basis for a purely monetary interest ultimately antagonistic to such development. This is paralleled by the fundamental internal contradiction (or, *antinomy*) of capitalist accumulation.

The conflict between these two tendencies usually erupts in an actually or potentially irrepressible form of contention only at those crisis-points of general monetary crisis at which the monetarist interest goes to the extreme in demanding negative rates of overall *real* capital formation. This monetary policy assumes such extremes under those conditions in which the accumulated debt-service payment of the society as a whole exceeds the monetary valuation of the surplus value produced. At such points, either a significant portion of the debt (at least) must be "triaged," or the monetarists' roll-over programs mean wars and-or the downward spiraling collapse of industry and agriculture. It is at such points, notably including the aftermath of the Napoleonic wars for England or the present global monetary crisis, that the anti-industrial fervor of the enraged monetarist interest is expressed by the strident advocacy of Malthusian or neo-Malthusian doctrines of "zero growth."

If a purely industrial-capitalist tendency prevailed, at such points the capitalist class would uniformly effect a comprehensive financial reorganization (debt moratoria, debt-discounting, and debt repudiations) adequate to serve the industrialist interest. It is at such points that the capitalist political forces representing an axiomatically anti-development, pro-monetarist tendency erupt as a most viable distinct faction within the capitalist class.

U.S. history is, not accidentally, one of the best sources for study of such conflicting tendencies. The American Revolution itself is the prime illustration. *(20)* The conflict between Alexander Hamilton and Aaron Burr, the conflict between the Federalists and Whigs, on the one side, and, on the other, the New York City-centered, Rothschild-linked forces of Martin van Buren and August Belmont, concerning the Third National Bank and similar issues, are also exemplary.

The hostility of leading European capitalist factions to the policies of the "Trilateral" Carter cabal are a fresh illustration of the same persisting conflict of tendencies within overall capitalist development.

It ought to be conceded that insofar as Marx's *Capital* and other writings tend toward the systematic error of equating British capitalist development with capitalist development in general, Marx's work is permeated with a corresponding collateral error. Purging Marx's work of such error at each appropriate point leaves the residue essentially intact as a scientific source-work.

---

20 Cf., *draft Constitution of the U.S. Labor Party.*

Luxemburg's Dissertation

Most narrowly considered, the analysis of Luxemburg's doctoral dissertation shows that all of the guiding criteria represented in her later writings were already established in relatively matured form by the end of the 1890s. If the dissertation is taken as an added point of reference for identifying the characteristic distinguishing features of her outlook and motivation, then the continuum of the principal factional disputes in which she was engaged within the international social-democracy is properly coherently re-examined as a whole in terms of the underlying, opposing characteristic philosophical world-outlooks of her principal opponents.

With that undertaking in view, it is useful as well as proper to regard her doctoral dissertation as, in an important sense, an autobiographical work. It reflects her point of view as that of a brilliant figure from an assimilated Jewish family situated within the environmental influences of late nineteenth century urban Polish culture. Given her disseration's description of the immediate history of Poland during her parents' lifetimes, it is useful that the student recognize in her environmentally conditioned viewpoint the basis for making a significant parallel among Luxemburg, Thomas Gresham, Hamilton's Federalism, and Fremont's Republican Party of the 1850s. In short, Luxemburg reflected the anti-aristocratic outlook appropriate to rapidly changing urban life on the (Eastern) *frontier* of European capitalist development.

Profoundly insightful in her contempt for the brutish romantic nationalism of the decayed Polish aristocracy (and of other admirers of the bestiality of Polish rural life), her *Polish pride of origins* is expressed in a focus upon the discovered world-historical achievements of nineteenth century Poland in bringing capitalist development to the brutish Russian Empire as a whole. This dominant sense of world-historical perspective reflects her position as the paragon among her close collaborators, the elite of that remarkable institution the Socialist Party of the Kingdoms of Poland and Lithuania (SDKPiL). In the best sense of such a characterization, the leading SDKPiL cadres were predominantly the sort of self-conscious intellectual elite most probably found on the various geographical and intellectual frontiers of general human progress.

She was imbued with the Idea of Progress in all its recaptured passion and comprehensiveness from the best aspects of the Renaissance and Enlightenment, and thus most agreeably predisposed to understand the same form of commitment as it was expressed by Karl Marx. What a gulf of difference in intellect and temperament separating Luxemburg from the stodgy, stultifying, petty "thoroughness" permeating the German Social-Democracy's bureaucracy!

The two principal figures of the pre-1918 SPD, Luxemburg and August Bebel, had nothing in common to ordinarily bring them into association. Only a François Rabelais perhaps could adequately portray the clownish philistine spectacle the SPD leadership represented by contrast with her. She was, as her worst SPD opponents suspected, an alien point of view which had thrust itself hubristically into their midst.

It is a simple matter of record, she thrust herself into the German Social-Democracy as soon as she had completed her doctoral dissertation, not because she admired the SPD, but because that party held hegemony over the international social-democracy. As she emphasized to her collaborator Jogiches, it was no good fighting issues only on the periphery of the socialist movement; one must move directly into the center of power and seize one's principal opponents directly by the ears. The SPD was a means for situating herself at the center of international socialist leadership — not because she was "power hungry," but because the international socialist policy was wrong and she must directly repair the situation. (In this sense, there is an instructive similarity between Luxemburg and a Lenin moving directly to seize leadership position on the Russian socialist leadership from under Plekhanov's nose.)

Europeans might have said of Rosa Luxemburg during 1898-1899: "What typically American hubris!" Such an epithet would have been, in a certain sense, fruitful.

This was not the first time Rosa Luxemburg had grabbed international socialist leaders by the ears. She had already had the international leadership by the ears over the question of Polish nationalism. As she entered the SPD, she immediately kicked a reluctant center leadership, including the party's founders, Wilhelm Liebknecht and August Bebel, into supporting her rip-roaring factional assault on Bernstein and Fabian influences. From that moment, until the Bolshevik Revolution, she was in fact the intellectual leader of the Marxist "left" in the international social-democracy as a whole.

In this process, she became preponderantly a German in fact as well as in citizenship. However, it should be emphasized that her roots to this effect were pre-1848 Enlightenment Germany, not the stultified post-1848 Germany licking the jackboot of cabbage-junker romanticism. Not the Germany which had pathetically retreated from the 1848 barricades, and in that process retraced its cultural traditions from Hegel, Heine, and Marx to the sentimental *Kitsch* of Klopstock and the brothers Schlegel.

In this overall process her intellectual connections to Karl Marx were essentially directly, rather than being her differentiation of the German Social-Democracy's presumed "orthodoxy." In such matters, the lineage of thought is sometimes determined not so much by one's immediate teachers as by the philosophical outlook which controls the student's selection of what he will or will not tolerate from instructors. The direct comparison of her doctoral dissertation with the later major writings helps to develop that point.

The principal analytical characteristic of Luxemburg's dissertation is its regulation by that same conception of capitalist expanded reproduction later elaborated in her *Accumulation of Capital*. The principal distinguishable elements of that conception are as follows:

First, she defines capitalist development as a process primarily associated with the realization of produced *real* social surplus in the interconnected forms of industry and urban culture and the capitalist transformation of agricultural production.

Second, she delimits successful realization of social surplus to the case of the spread of successive layers of relatively more-advanced productive technology to subsume, assimilate, and supersede less-advanced forms of productive technology.

Third, she conditionally unifies these two conceptions into the approximation of a single primary conception, by making rising social productivity through technologically oriented increases in per capita real capital fórmation the, in effect, unified, "non-linear" parameter of overall capitalist development.

Fourth, she unconditionally qualifies that primary parameter to include the necessity of both the cultural advancement of the material and intellectual life of the working-class household, and emphasizes that this is the constant precondition (as a secular tendency) for effective assimilation of new technologies, to the effect of enabling rising social productivity.

Fifth, she emphasizes the expanding, interdependent international division of labor as the primary correlative of effective capitalist development.

Sixth, she deprecates the monetary aspect of capitalist development to the status of a necessary secondary feature of *real* capitalist development as such.

As a correlated notion, she also regards nationalism as a brutish anachronism *relative to* the current capitalist development of the international productive forces. She does not arbitrarily reject nationalism, but reduces its role to that of a vestige which can not be shucked arbitrarily from humanity all at once. She delimits the vestigial positive role of national struggles to the historically circumscribed mediating function of realizing the potential world-historical role of national political force in behalf of general human progress.

These are the common, central features of her dissertation and those later writings to be grouped with the *Accumulation of Capital*.

In economics, Luxemburg's most notable points of difference in her *Accumulation* with Lenin and others was twofold. First, she understood and emphasized that the realization of social surplus was not a peculiarity of capitalist production, but a characteristic feature of overall human development, hence a primary feature of human culture. *(21)* Second, she emphasized

---

21 Cf., *Accumulation*, p. 317, n. 1 (on Ilyin). "...the same author is responsible for the statement that enlarged reproduction begins only with capitalism. It quite escapes him that under conditions of simple reproduction, which he takes to be the rule for all pre-capitalist modes of production, we should probably never have advanced beyond the stage of the paleolithic scraper." It is notable that Luxemburg selects that 1899 passage from Lenin during 1912, and that such a criticism of Lenin's economic-theoretical blundering (e.g., *Imperialism*) is appropriate to the Lenin of the World War I period.

that the *secular* tendency for rising material preconditions of cultural development of households, despite tolerable historically brief exceptions (primitive accumulation), was an indispensable condition for successful continuation of capitalist and related forms of economic development.

The direct comparison of Luxemburg with Lenin is generally the most fruitful initial approach to analysis. The fact that they agreed in crucial features of their personal political worldoutlook has the greatest advantages for assessing their specific disagreements in points associated with the Luxemburg case more generally.

Lenin and Luxemburg were broadly commonly distinguished from nearly all the other prominent figures of the early twentieth century socialist movement as thorough *voluntarists*. With Lenin, this developed outlook is properly studied from the reference-standpoint of Chernyshevsky. Lenin, philosophically also a product of the Eastern frontier of European capitalist development, chose the voluntarist Chernyshevskian current of Russian socialism over the alternative, fatalistic currents of Rothschild political agent Herzen.

This connection is emphasized by various features of Lenin's political-psychological profile. The very title of his *What Is To Be Done?* The embedded voluntarist impulsions compelling his break with the relatively fatalistic Plekhanov. His constant focus upon the problem of "Oblomovism" within the ranks of Russian socialists. His characteristic policy, in politics as such, for seeking out some striking innovation in insight and policy which was at the same time coherent with the lawful ordering of social processes.

This same Leninist quality carried over into the best among the distinguishing features of the Bolsheviks. The essential underlying philosophical difference between the Bolsheviks and the Mensheviks was the difference earlier exhibited between Chernyshevsky and Herzen. It is useful in this connection to see the Soviet industrialization process as a realization of the impulses elaborated in Chernyshevsky's relevant writings. It is also pertinent that the leading Menshevik theoreticians subsequently, and correctly so, identified Leninist *voluntarism* as the epistemological root-cause of their fundamental differences with the Bolsheviks.

Lenin's voluntarism did not carry over effectively into his conceptions of theoretical economics. In this domain, he was relatively a Menshevik of the *post hoc ergo propter hoc* school of analysis of capitalist development per se. This led him to the exaggerated misconceptions, of mechanistic specificity of capitalist development for which Luxemburg rightly ridiculed him *(22)* , and to the more significantly elaborated blunders pervading his *Imperialism*.

It is otherwise necessary at least to identify the other most famous category of differences between Luxemburg and Lenin. Each proceeded from a primary commitment to a voluntarist outlook to a different conclusion; this cites the widely misrepresented fact of the actual differences between Luxemburg and Lenin respecting "spontaneity" versus "centralization." Although Luxemburg correctly emphasized the educational-experiential process of transforming a fragmented working class into a *class-for-itself* (i.e., her "mass strike" analysis), she *underestimated* the importance of an independent political force, centralized in form, as the institutionalized agent for programmatically guiding the masses' education. Lenin, who underestimated the specifics of the class-for-itself process, and who thus overestimated the *spontaneous* radicalism of the fragmented working-class forces, oversimplified the notion of effectiveness of a centralized executive agency.

Their convergence in such matters is shown most directly during and immediately following the Russian and Polish upsurges of 1905, including Lenin's support for Luxemburg's "mass strike" thesis in the international social-democracy. Their divergence shows in connection with the German question during the 1918-1919 period, in which Lenin grossly misestimated the "spontaneous" readiness of the German workers to respond to the Bolshevik revolution, whereas Luxemburg relatively correctly assessed the process *needed* to produce a viable mass-based split from the old social-democracy.

The outcome of their included differences was shaped by the circumstances of the formation of the Communist International. The leading Bolshevik circles included a high proportion of individuals hostile to Luxemburg's outlook (e.g., L.

---

22 *ibid*.

Trotsky) *(23)*, and individuals and currents which carried into Bolshevism some of the worst features of the utopian-reductionism traditions of the social-democracy. This was complicated by the interventions of predominantly British agents working within leading and other circles of the Bolsheviks as well as other elements of the Communist International. Karl Radek, Bukharin, G. Zinoviev are exemplary of the Bolsheviks responsible for the pogrom against "Luxemburgism," while Fabian agents such as Karl Korsch and the lunatic ultra-lefts are properly prominently included among the wretches who furthered this pogrom in the German and other Communist parties. *(24)*

In sum, Lenin's own weakness, his susceptibility to the same reductionist misrepresentation of Marx's economics and method otherwise predominant in the social-democracy, became the added means by which "Luxemburgism" was fraudulently "contained" and then extirpated as an intellectual current within the post-1921 socialist movement.

This aspect of the matter reflects in part the circumstances

---

23 The fact that wretches such as Karl Korsch and Korsch's cronies lumped Luxemburg and Trotsky together in the inquisitions of the 1920s German Communist circles has produced wishful efforts to find some special convergence between Trotskyism and Luxemburgism. This enterprise appears to be favored by the fact that both Luxemburg and Trotsky were extraordinarily brilliant intellectual spokesmen of Eastern European Jewish backgrounds. This enterprise appears to be warranted in substance, at least superficially, by the fact that Trotsky arrived, presumably independently, at a simplified version of Luxemburg's earlier "permanent revolution" conceptions. Hence, such well-wishers are astonished to discover that in reality Trotksy and Luxemburg were mutually acquainted, and decidedly not friendly.

Essentially, Luxemburg distrusted the pre-World War I Trotsky for the same reasons that Lenin did. The reasons for this distrust are aptly identified by referring to a small but positively symptomatic obscenity Trotsky contributed to *Vienna Pravda*. In the course of lambasting one of the labile Adler's newest chimeras — which any sensible individual could have found fresh reason to undertake any given Wednesday morning in Old Vienna — Trotksy exploits that ritual chore to the included point of praising the "finished proletarian leadership" of the SPD. This is the sort of shameless opportunism on Trotsky's part which disgusted both Lenin and Luxemburg; yet, apart from being downright nauseating in its own right (considering what Trotsky said privately concerning the philistinism of the SPD leadership), it reflected a specific political tendency within Trotsky. If Trotsky was not characteristically soft toward utopian *doctrines*, etc., he was recurrently soft toward anarchosyndicalists, "proletarian kernel" centrists and ultra-lefts.

24 The pogrom against "Luxemburgism" was launched by British intelligence and allied circles through such instruments as Karl Radek and the German "ultra-lefts." From behind the scenes, the constant stoking of this pogrom-campaign was coordinated by Karl Korsch. It is not irrelevant that the two key Bolsheviks responsible for this filth were Karl Radek and Bukharin, both pre-war and war-time protégés of super-agent Parvus.

of formation of the Communist International. The strategic desperation of the Bolsheviks impelled them to grant membership franchises to almost any forces which could be mobilized for a committed struggle against both the imperialists and the imperialists' social-democratic allies. In this way, hordes, relatively speaking, of anarchosyndicalists and other ultra-left successors of lunatic utopianism were ingested into the French, German and other newly formed Communist parties. This ironically laid the basis for the principal internal subversions of the Communist International by British and allied political intelligence agencies. It also meant that the very Communist International for which Luxemburgism had become de facto an integral part had adopted a philosophical policy of keeping a foot in each of the scientific and utopian socialist traditions, so resurrecting among the Communists a new form of the same unprincipled combination which had characterized the centrists of the old social-democracy.

The primary characteristic of the "ultra-left" or lunatic socialist is an axiomatic preoccupation with two interconnected premises. On the one side, the lunatic socialist is concerned with issues of "redistribution." If he tolerates broader "socialist" demands than those, such broader notions are regarded essentially as inductive generalizations from the laundry-list of localized "redistributionist" demands, and are regarded as relatively ineffable and even downright alien to the extent that they not simply give a rhetorical appearance of moralizing generality to localized, "practical" redistributionist issues. On the other side, the lunatic socialist regards socialism and the "class struggle" as axiomatically derived from the "horny hand of labor." The lunatic socialist presumes that the "workers" individually secrete class consciousness from their circumstances and experience in day-to-day struggles over wages, working conditions, and so forth, and that socialism is simply the intensification and extrapolation of local wildcat strikes over such issues to a society-wide political struggle for such demands in general.

For such reasons, with important momentary exceptional cases, the socialist movement within the industrialized capitalist nations has not been effective, except as a *meliorist* force within capitalist political processes. Acting, for reasons given, as an essentially anti-socialist force, reenforcing anarchoid morality and perspectives among workers, as a revolutionary socialist force that movement has been predominantly a bad joke.

In the United States in particular, we see the outcome of that sickness of utopian traditions most clearly by drawing up a list of avowedly socialist organizations: the Communist Party U.S.A., the Socialist Workers Party (the traditional "Trotskyist" flagship organization), the sundry "Trotskyist" and "Maoist" cults, plus the outright anarchists and anarchosyndicalists, are all aligned on the side of the neo-Malthusian policies centered in the "left" aspect of the cabal around Jimmy Carter. They are committed to "redistributions of goodies" under circumstances of de-industrialization, collapse of total essential social services, and so forth.

This contrasts to the same ultimate conclusion with the performance of socialist currents in Western Europe. There, just because pro-industrialist factions of capitalist forces have dug in their heels in opposition to *Carterista* global austerity and probable thermonuclear holocaust, a large component of the socialist parties, notably including the Communist Party of Italy, have aligned themselves with the pro-industrial capitalist factions in a common national and global self-interest.

Inverting this observation of fact, to thus arrive at the relevant causal connections, one must properly inquire what the effect must have been had Luxemburg's *Accumulation* theses been directly debated, to the effect that such a debate would have shaped the intellectual climate of policy-formulation within the pre-1917 international social-democracy? Would the German worker, in particular, have agreed with the notion of a national policy in which continued technological advancement advanced his practiced skill and increased his material conditions of household life? If the debate had progressed to such obvious expressions of the issues at stake, what must have resulted? The socialist movement, or at least a large component of it enjoying varying degrees of actual and imminent mass support, must have immediately allied with the pro-industrial interest against the monetarist interest, and proceeded thence toward a class-for-itself socialist perspective.

The relevant problem of the individual working man or woman is that he or she is estranged from sensuous connections to the determining overall process in which, for example, general prosperity and depressions are commonly determined. So alienated, his conscious practical self-interest, his sensuous perception of self-interest, is restricted to those immediate social relations within which he believes that he has the actual or reasonably potential means for altering his immediate circumstances. As long as this arrangement persists, such a brutalized, heteronomic worker is intellectually relatively susceptible to the currents of "socialism" derived from the utopian tradition.

There are two complementary circumstances in which this arrangement is altered. To the extent that individual workers or strata of workers are intellectually advanced in their development, as for the included cases of skilled workers and technicians, such individuals and groups are intellectually capable of comprehending the way in which the practical interconnections of an economy as a whole interreact with the acts and circumstances of local and individual life. They are capable of *theoretically* escaping the brutalized mental outlook appropriate to lunatic-socialist propaganda and so forth. Otherwise, the emergence of generalized political upsurges, in which the individualized worker is thus connected to a mass institution of generalized capability, causes the masses of ordinary workers to become capable of beginning to comprehend the sensuous actuality of a primary general social interest.

For such reasons, and related reasons, the scientific socialist current always re-originates as the initiating effort of handfuls of extraordinarily gifted intellectuals, such as Karl Marx or Rosa Luxemburg. The question, whether that initiating leads toward a mass socialist movement, is a practical question of the process governing the influence of the ideas radiating from those exceptional individuals. Conversely, as such intellectuals threaten to intrude into the social base controlled by opposing forces, the process takes the forms of either a factional conflict of ideas or, black-propaganda slanders and other covert and semi-covert "dirty tricks" employed by the opponents in the effort to avoid a debate they fear they must lose.

That, as the translator has outlined the record of the debate over Luxemburg in her accompanying preface, is the gist of the way in which Luxemburg's conceptions point directly to the nature of the utopian-Fabian and centrist (one foot in each camp) opposition dividing the social-democracy and also the Communist International. From that to uncovering the dualism of the capitalist factions is a short quick step.

Summary Argument

We have established the leading points bearing upon the use of the Luxemburg case to the end of, immediately, exposing the existence and characteristic interaction of two mutually irreconcilable tendencies within the 1898-1921 social-democracy and emerging Communist International. We have, similarly, outlined the connection between such a demonstration and evidence which overthrows the prevailing assumptions of the old political science doctrines in general. Now, we summarize the proof.

The procedure begins with the identification of the characteristic of Rosa Luxemburg's philosophical-political profile at two relevant points of her leading role within the social-democracy: at the outset of her recognized leading political position, the turn of the century, and during the factional disputes leading toward the war and the split in the social-democracy, 1912-1916. Her doctoral dissertation (complementary to her *Reform or Revolution?* of the same period), and her *Accumulation of Capital* are adopted as the most appropriate literary references for establishing the profile at those successive points.

At both points, Luxemburg is established as a humanist, so characterized by the "Idea of Progress" as the proper name for all her criteria of. judgment in politics and morality. Her humanism is also characterized by axiomatic commitment to the *voluntarist* notion of *lawful freedom* specific to humanist currents. Otherwise, the characteristic economic-theoretical and political axioms of her outlook at both points are the same; between the two points, there is significant development, but no alteration of the axiomatic features of her philosophical world-outlook.

The doctoral dissertation (directly to be compared with the *Reform or Revolution?* from the same period) gives a latest date for the original appearance of her characteristic outlook and economic-theoretical method. It also points directly — because of its unavoidable autobiographical features — to the context for her unusual development as being the Eastern frontier of urban culture for general European capitalist development.

In her doctoral dissertation (as also in *Reform or Revolution?*) she rejects the empiricist and related notions of ideas. A fact, or idea, for her is manifestly the conception which corresponds to an operative unifying principle. Her concern, directly emphasized as the overall thesis of the dissertation, is to first determine the extent of the factual domain which must be taken *as a whole* to avoid the otherwise inevitable fallacy of composition—or, to avoid what Spinoza characterizes as "fictitious" knowledge. The consequent, overall first conclusion of her thesis is the demonstration that the nineteenth century relationship between Poland and Russia is governed in all its distinguishable characteristic features and apparent paradoxes by the leading role of Czarist Polish capitalist development in mediating the capitalist development of Russia. In turn, she demonstrates that the capitalist development of Poland and Russia as a unified process is subsumed by international capitalist development in general, and must be examined within the frame of reference of overall international capitalist develpment.

Her axiomatic criteria for *development* are those derivations of the humanist Idea of Progress we have identified as prominent within the dissertation: The realization of social surplus as technologically advanced industrial expansion, capitalist transformation of agricultural productive relations and modes of production, and a secular tendency for improved material and other household preconditions of rising social productivity, through a culturally advancing labor force.

Once she has established the general conclusions to this effect, she tests those general conclusions against the apparent contradictory phenomena: the fact of nationalism and so forth. Out of the interconnection between such comprehended apparent anomalies and the general principles, she elaborates the process or development associated with "tension" between the general and particulars in that form.

This is most directly relevant to the contrasting fact that the German social-democracy was under the partly explicit, partly half-conscious influence of neo-Kantianism generally, and the banalities of Friedrich Lange more emphatically. To this must be added the important qualification that the prevailing neo-

Kantian doctrines were in fact anti-Kant respecting the issue of *heteronomy*. Whereas Kant emphasized that heteronomic wilfulness was the fundamental pathology in human behavior, the politically influential currents of so-called neo-Kantianism actually represented the contrary views as expressed by Fichte and such silly Kantian epigonoi as the ignorant Fries. This pseudo-Kantian and neo-Kantian "materialist" outlook in Germany and Austria was the continental philosophical correlative and cousin for Fabian utilitarianism-empiricism in English-speaking culture. (Pragmatism, the utilitarian degeneracy of neo-Kantianism, is the form in which English-speaking culture pathetically emulated the superior philosophical literacy of Germany.)

Hence, as Marx's own writings illuminate the same conflict, Luxemburg's encounter with the social-democracy generally was directly an irreconcilable conflict between her partially replicated, partially assimilated commitment to the Marxian dialectical outlook (*perfection* as a self-subsisting positive universal principle, to emphasize the traditional humanist setting of that outlook), against the hereditary outgrowths of the utopian current. This was, and always is, the form of the correlated philosophical expression of the conflict between the pro-development and pro-monetarist factions in politics.

In respect to the turn-of-the-century "revisionism" debate, it must be understood that the misrepresentation of that debate as a defense of social-democratic "orthodoxy" is more or less typical of the way in which most factional affrays are misunderstood by most of the participants, from the standpoint of *false consciousness*. Since the mediating motivating force for winning factional positions in organizations is the members' social ties to the organization as an institution, it is more or less inevitable that the symptomatic, deceptive principle of "legitimacy" or "orthodoxy" should be employed as a rhetorical factional device by at least one and usually all factions.

The practical correlatives of the "nationalism debate" in the Polish and Russian socialist movements are in direct correspondence with the issues of the "revisionism" debate within the SPD.

In opposition to Luxemburg's thesis, concerning the world-historical role of Polish urban developments under the Czar for world capitalist development and Russian capitalist development, her socialist opponents offered two more or less distinct defenses of simple-minded nationalism. The (later) proto-fascist Pilsudski, et al. expressed the bucolic romanticism of the Polish aristocracy, as mediated through the romanticism of urban petit-bourgeois and allied circles. The other pro-nationalist faction, typified by the Russian social-democracy and pre-war Bolsheviks, proceeded from an apparent unwillingness to break entirely with the fatalism of Herzen, et al. They fed this backwardness variously by a concern to adapt to the romantic sentiments of the politically more backward Russian workers, and by an otherwise commendable hostility toward the oppression of national minorities under Czarism.

Luxemburg and her SDKPiL collaborators expressed the outlook on Russia otherwise expressed, as she emphasizes in the dissertation, of the most advanced Polish capitalists: the decisive role of Russian markets for Polish urban progress, and the need to maintain and develop the immediate division of labor among developing Polish and Russian industries. Like Marx, Luxemburg expressed the standpoint of *permanent revolution*, a political working-class struggle for capitalist industrial and agricultural development under republican political forms, *going over organically* to the political continuation of that process as a socialist economic development.

Her opponents argued for the specificity of "stages of national development" within the relatively hermetic framework of populations and associated areas characterized by an existing commonality of language and "national culture." Lenin was most prominent among those who combined Luxemburg's thrust toward permanent revolution (e.g., *Two Tactics*) with an unwillingness to break entirely from the pro-nationalist social-democratic scholasticisms of Plekhanov, et al.

In historical fact, the immediate authorship of the nationalism doctrines for the Polish and Russian socialist movements was the leadership of the Austrian social-democracy. The Austrian social-democracy thus visibly exhibited itself as the socialist arm of the Hapsburg Vienna bureaucracy, whose goal was the maintenance of the Austro-Hungarian Empire through policies of "cultural relativism" akin to British colonial and imperialist policies for the colonial and semi-colonial world.

LUXEMBURG AND THE CRISIS IN POLITICAL SCIENCE

This Austrian social-democratic kinship to the doctrines of the British Foreign Office was no coincidence. The fatalist socialist currents in Russian life were the direct outgrowth of the sponsored influence of such Russian British political agents as Herzen, who the Rothschilds and others had funded and otherwise aided against the voluntarist socialist current typified by Chernyshevsky. Otherwise, since the days of Rothschild puppet Metternich, and the general British agent of influence, the Holy Alliance in general, the British policies of "cultural relativism" (imposed relative cultural backwardness) had been the characteristic policies of all British continental agents and the Austrian regime in particular.

As later exemplified by World Federalism, and by the articulation of one-world ravings of the Fabian Bertrand Russell, the persisting perspective of the British monetarist faction and the contemporary Atlanticists has been to establish Atlanticist one-world rule in a "neo-colonialist" form significantly resembling the old Austro-Hungarian Empire: each nation to enjoy its own hermetic "cultural autonomy," and thus become a correspondingly impotent component of a confederation effectively ruled by a supra-national imperium.

The direct connection between the nationalist currents of Polish and Russian socialist movements and British Foreign Office activities is underlined by the 1916 proposal of Parvus to the Kaiser's intelligence services. This 1916 proposal echoed and paralleled essentially identical British Fabian policies for Eastern Europe.

Nationalism was to be fostered in Eastern Europe by the German (and British) political intelligence services, to the effect of balkanizing all Eastern Europe, and specifically splitting the Russian Empire among a Finnish, Polish, Baltic, Great Russian, and Ukrainian separate states, giving the British (e.g., the Rothschilds) direct puppet-state control of Ukrainian wheat and Caucasus petroleum. That Parvus, a Fabian agent since 1893, a political intelligence operative for British armaments interests, and an agent for Rothschild grain cartels, should have peddled such a British policy to the German high command in 1916, exemplifies the reality operating.

It was this same Parvus, operating with the aid of his paid agent, Karl Radek, and other protégés (such as Bukharin,

Riazanov) in the effort to manipulate Lenin as an unwitting destabilization agent of both German and British Russian projects, who engineered the "sealed train" and funding, and whose prestige came abruptly to decline through the unexpected autumn 1917 consequences of Lenin's return to Russia.

Luxemburg's policy-thrust was for a *programmatically unified* continental socialist movement, for which the common programmatic-strategic effort of the German, Polish and Russian socialist movements was crucial. This was a commitment to the socialist form of capitalist economic development of Poland and Russia, mediated significantly through eastward orientation of German industrial capital exports. This aspect of her policy, which became not only a clear policy but a probably realizable alternative after 1905, prompted her former centrist factional allies (including British spy August Bebel) to launch the "containment" effort against her from 1906 onwards. It was this powerful feature of Luxemburg's policy, plus the Bolshevik example of autumn 1917, which inclusively prompted the Anglo-American Armistice Commission to order the Ebert government to effect her assassination in January 1919, and caused such Anglo-American agents as Karl Radek, Karl Korsch and others to push for the pogrom against "the virus of Luxemburgism" after her death.

The interaction between Luxemburg and the turn-of-the-century social-democracy was determined in the following principal way:

Beginning with the 1877-1886 mass-strike waves in the United States, the same general upsurge spread into Europe during the last half of the 1880s, notably England and Germany. Despite Bebel's efforts to undermine the German strikes, the strikes toppled Bismarck, overturned the Bismarckian anti-socialist laws, and vastly augmented the German social-democracy's membership with new layers of workers and others. These new forces were thus inclusively characterized by the influence of a mass-strike experience. This shift in embedded philosophical outlook among a portion of the SPD's membership forced the accomodation of the SPD leadership to this development.

The immediate formal result was the replacement of the Gotha program by the 1891 Erfurt program. In the latter draft, Kautsky provided something for each of the two opposing currents within the SPD. For the old, meliorist, hereditarily utopian SPD leaderships, he established the utopian outlook as the practical philosophical premise of party life. For the consoling edification of the currents verging upon the Marxian outlook, he provided ineffable rhetorical echoes of the *Communist Manifesto*, the so-called "maximum program." This Erfurt "judo" approach to containment of the sociologically pro-Marxist current was not yet consolidated until after the turn of the century, not until the establishment of the covert alliance between Bebel and the German General Trade-Union Commission established on the model of the British Fabian experiences.

Luxemburg's intervention during 1898-1899 was in effect a direct attack on the philosophical rationalization for the "minimum program," in behalf of the actuality nominally tolerated through the "maximum program." She succeeded to the extent that Bebel and Kautsky could be inspired to prevent a too-blatant emphasis on the utopian-meliorist current (typified by Bernstein's theses) from splitting the SPD into its two constituent currents. She failed to the extent that the same Bebel and Kautsky then subsequently responded to prevent the limited success of Luxemburg's effort from leading to the extirpation of the Bernsteinist current.

This issue became clearer during the "mass strike" debate, and the continuing factional struggles between Luxemburg and the centrists throughout the pre-war period.

In *Accumulation* and associated writings, Luxemburg extended her systematic attack against British-centered monetarist factions, by showing that imperialism did not represent capitalism's embedded thrust for global development of the productive forces, but represented predominantly a monetarist policy of imposed relative cultural and economic backwardness. Imperialism was a perpetuation of the primitive-accumulation looting expressed in the policies of the Fuggers and other mercantilists of the Hapsburg period of the sixteenth and early seventeenth century economic collapse of continental Europe.

Apart from Luxemburg, the remainder of the socialist movement predominantly defended British monetarism, to the extent of representing it as nothing but a lawful continuation of capitalist industrializing impulses. This inevitably reflected itself in the economic-theoretical form of defending monetarism as an intrinsically capitalist policy, and of denying therefore the existence of any fundamental contradiction-in-fact in nineteenth century capitalist accumulation. In terms of economic-theoretical formalities, Hilferding, Bukharin, Otto Bauer, and also Lenin threw out both Marx's "Internal Contradictions" chapters from Volume III of *Capital*, and with that the notion of the primary role of *necessity-freedom* as elaborated in the concluding section (Section VII) of that same volume.

In the overall development of the dispute, it must be emphasized that the apparently abstract ideas which factions and movements profess correspond (in the main) to rationalizations for the day-to-day practice and associated practical criteria of actual social forces. Such rationalizations not only reflect the underlying practical considerations, but, as rationalizations, perform an indispensable sociological function. They reenforce the adherence to the practical criteria employed by the constituent individuals and small groupings of such a persuasion. The abstract rationalizations, as they are the accepted ideology of a movement or faction, give a wanted legitimacy of generally accepted moral principles to the otherwise heteronomic impulsions of the constituents. Thus, an attack upon the abstract generalizations portends a responding enraged defense of such mere abstractions, whenever the constituents become consciously or semi-consciously sensible that the *legitimacy* of their localist, day-to-day practical impulses is being placed into jeopardy.

This corresponds to the history of factional struggles. As a factional dispute among a handful arouses at least semi-conscious awareness of such underlying connections among broader forces the factional affray accelerates. In the course of its elaboration, the affray arrives asymptotically at such actual splits and other manifest forms as might have appeared merely to be a remote possible implication at the outset of the dispute.

Such appreciations are properly rule-of-thumb matters to those who have both closely studied factional disputes within the socialist organizations from the vantage-point of having participated as leading proponents in a few themselves. It is proverbial second-nature for such a person to ask his opponents: "*Why* do you push that point?'' "To *what* practical end are you so strongly urging that issue?"

It is rather the *academic* political science view, to which political factional developments are relatively abstract contemplations, by which this insight is generally overlooked. The academic political science figure exaggerates the independent importance of formal ideas-in-themselves, undoubtedly because his immediate social position is affected principally by the relative academic authority of this or that mere abstract interpretation of ideas. In the real world, who is *formally* right or wrong (in the academic sense) has less enduring importance; the important thing is the practical ends to which the application of ideas leads.

So, given the cited circumstances of dualism which Luxemburg's factional efforts intersected within the socialist movement of her time, a practical assessment of disputes directly exposes the existance and implications of the two principal currents.

This evaluation is not speculative, but corresponds exactly to the experience of the Labor Committees' development since late 1965.

Up to autumn 1965, this writer was unacquainted with any of Rosa Luxemburg's writings but her *Reform or Revolution?* That regrettable avoidance was a result of his credulous acceptance of the prevailing reputation of her theoretical accomplishments among both socialists and academic political science circles generally. Hence, this writer's own development, which was completed in all its essential economic-theoretical and methodological features before that time, occurred without a direct influence by Luxemburg.

However, fortuitously impelled to take up her *Accumulation* and other writings at the end of 1965, he found coincidences in economic-theoretical views which situated him closer to Luxemburg than any other socialist figure since Karl Marx. As the Labor Committees were developed from scratch, beginning mid-1966, the examination of the history of the socialist movement, and then history more generally, from the vantage-point of seeking reasons why the relatively correct economic theoretical views of so prominent an authority as Luxemburg had been so idiotically deprecated, provided the stimulus and key to uncovering, first, the real history of the modern socialist movement, and from that standpoint of reference the real history of capitalist development.

It was this directed activity, both its immediate fruits, and the critical attitude it fostered for other areas of investigation, which contributed more than anything but the Labor Committees' essential methodological outlook to the relatively unprecedented and expanding catalytic influence of the Labor Committees as an intellectual force in global political developments today. Hence, the thesis submitted in this introduction is essentially a summation of something already accomplished, a proposal that broader layers replicate this to secure similar benefits for themselves.

Lyndon H. LaRouche Jr.
New York City
Dec. 15, 1976

Translator's Preface

Rosa Luxemburg's doctoral dissertation, *The Industrial Development of Poland*, was written and read as one of her most important pieces of political weaponry in a years-long political battle that had already brought her international recognition as a socialist leader. The issue of that battle was progress, and here the young Luxemburg sets out the principle of progress, of development, that was the conceptual basis for her unequalled leading role in the working-class movement.

It remains the dividing line that separates Luxemburg and her heirs from the monetarist enemies of capitalist and socialist progress alike who murdered Luxemburg and have since strived to murder her intellectual legacy as well. That Luxemburg's first major work, one of the best examples of economic history ever written, is only appearing in English translation today, nearly 80 years after its original German publication, indicates the success of this campaign of suppression. Now, however, the availability of *The Industrial Development of Poland* gives us a new and powerful piece of intellectual ammunition as that life and death battle approaches its conclusion.

The immediate (although not explicitly named) victim of Luxemburg's thesis was the Polish Socialist Party, her opponents in the Polish movement for much of her lifetime. In particular, her fire was aimed at the Polish Socialists' central argument that social revolution was out of the question for the Polish working class until after Poland's reunification and independence had been achieved. The international social-democracy's hallowed "theory of stages," the justification went, ensured that the further development of capitalism in Poland was not possible until the dream of independence became a reality.

Luxemburg's thesis, the first comprehensive economic history of Poland ever published, made mincemeat out of the "social patriot" theoreticians with a devastatingly thorough proof that Russian Poland's capitalist development, far from creating a "progressive nationalist bourgeoise," was integrating the Polish economy more and more completely with that of mother Russia; she locates this phenomenon as the necessary expression of capitalism's historic tendency toward greater and greater expansion, consolidation, and integration of the world's productive forces. With vivid irony, Luxemburg dissects the two-sidedness of capitalism — its global development of productive forces and its voracious destructiveness, its impetus to progress and its plunge toward complete bankruptcy. The working class' opposition to capitalism, she shows, must be based on superseding its advances while extirpating its barbarities, not on chasing fantasies of "national liberation" back into the far more horrible barbarities of pre-capitalism.

Even more important, *The Industrial Development of Poland* is clearly intended as a demonstration of actually Marxist method. The restrictions imposed by the academic niceties of a dissertation become for her an opportunity to show, with the socialist's political vocabulary set aside, that it is the coherence of the Marxist method with its subject, the process of humanity's — and in specific, capitalism's — forward development, that finally differentiates Marxism from the philistinism and agentry rampant in the social-democracy. "Outwardly it has adopted social-democratic terminology, swears by Marx and Engels, talks about class interests, about class struggle, about capitalist development," Luxemburg wrote of Polish Socialism in an article contemporaneous with her dissertation. "But what peeks out from under this revolutionary raiment is the reactionary cloven hoof of the petit bourgeoisie, the *opposition* to capitalist development, the interest of a layer which is itself impotent to champion its interests under its own banner."*

This is the source of the depth and ferociously uncompromising rigor of Luxemburg's work, beside which even the best of Luxemburg's contemporaries, Lenin for example, show themselves as intellectual minor-leaguers. How hideously typical it is of Rosa Luxemburg's posthumous career that this long and detailed work that predates by decades Lenin's celebrated overturn of the "theory of stages" and Trotsky's theory of "combined and uneven development" has had to wait so long for publication in English.

A New Political Universe

Luxemburg is best known for her achievements of the second half of her life — the battle against British agent Eduard Bernstein and the rest of the "revisionist" tendency, her role in the 1905 Russian Revolution and her mass strike perspective, the creation of Spartakus — and her murder on the orders of the German social-democracy's British overseers. Her earlier history shows graphically the confluence of personal and political development that shaped the woman who was the greatest socialist intellectual of her era.

Luxemburg had been active as a revolutionary socialist for at least ten years prior to the writing of her dissertation, with the beginnings of her life in politics concealed in the deliberate obscurity of Poland's clandestine revolutionary movement. She was born in the Russian section of Poland (called Congress Poland or the Kingdom of Poland) in the midst of the transition from the old Polish revolutionary movement to the new, from the republican nobility's battles for a free Poland to the rise of working-class socialism. The decade prior to her birth in 1871 saw the old Polish nationalist movement's last, hopeless efforts to overthrow Russian rule put down by a combination of brute force

---

*Emphases throughout are from the original.

and judiciously granted progressive reforms. A series of mass demonstrations and riots peaked in the January Insurrection of 1863, then flared and sputtered into nothingness over the next several years. In response, Russia tightened its grip on Congress Poland, while at the same time, undercutting the nationalist ferment's social basis, the nobility, by loosening the bonds of serfdom and pushing the Polish economy toward the modern world.

The year that Luxemburg was born, the Paris Commune rose as "the glorious harbinger of a new society" and of the new terms of class struggle. The same process made itself felt, slowly but inevitably, beneath the vigilantly policed surface of Polish political life. Luxemburg, the youngest child of an intellectually energetic and cosmopolitan middle-class family, was representative of the strata of Polish youth who grew up together with and into the new social-democratic movement.

The growth of conspiratorial Blanquist-type socialist groups in the 1870s culminated in the founding of the underground Proletariat organization in 1882. The new character of the movement was firmly stamped by a series of strikes the following year, including a mass strike in the vicinity of Warsaw (where the Luxemburgs lived) led by the Proletariat grouping. The revolutionaries soon received the full attention of the Czarist police, and by 1885 its top leaders had all been arrested and imprisoned and, in several cases, hung — the first death sentences carried out since the suppression of the 1863-64 uprising. It appears that Rosa Luxemburg's involvement in politics began here; the older grades of the Warsaw high schools were foci of covert political agitation and organizing. In her last year of high school, Luxemburg's activities helped lose her an academic prize and after her graduation in 1887, she worked actively with Proletariat.

In the article cited above, written ten years later for the *Sozialistische Monatshefte* on "Socialism in Poland," Luxemburg described Proletariat as "the first significant socialist organization which for years led the movement in Poland. Its physiognomy was determined by two different factors: on the one side, by the influence of the glorious Russian terrorist party 'Narodnaya Volya' and on the other side by that of the Western European workers' movement." Here were the two contradictory antipodes of the movement — the peasant's and the artisan's protest against the advance of capitalism, and the proletariat's fight to go beyond that advance by making it its own — and Proletariat embodied both. But because of the particularities of the Polish situation and the intellectual qualities of Proletariat's founder, Warynski, the tendency's best side was expressed in its stance toward the critical national question. "The founders of the Proletariat party," Luxemburg wrote, "even before they had given it a party organization, had made a sharp separation between the working-class movement and nationalism." Proletariat subscribed to the *Communist Manifesto*'s identification of the expansion of the capitalist order as the necessary precondition for a proletarian revolution, and defended the Polish working class' progressive identity against all the atavistic political currents demanding "national liberation." Wrote Warynski in 1881, "The explicit or veiled putting forward of such a program (for the restoration of Poland)...is *destructive* in view of the tasks which socialists must take into account in their activity...not 'national rebirth,' but the expansion of the political rights of the proletariat, making possible a mass organization for the battle with the bourgeoisie as a political and social class." This Luxemburg termed "Proletariat's most lasting service to the Polish working class."

The other side of the coin was the group's conspiratorial methods and "exemplary terrorism," to which it clung in common with the explicitly pro-feudal Russian Narodnaya Volya. But the explosion of spontaneous strikes in 1887 and 1888 and the rapid growth of the core of a mass working-class organization gave an entirely new, social-democratic character to the Polish movement. "A new generation of socialists put itself at the helm of the trade-union struggle," Luxemburg wrote. She and her closest political collaborators were the leaders of that new generation.

Into the International Arena

The police did not look kindly on such developments, however, and Proletariat was subjected to severe repression. After the rounding up of its leaders in 1886, the organization dissolved into individual cells and sub-groups, while the police continued to hunt down its members. By 1889, Luxemburg had come to their attention, and the 18-year-old girl had to escape arrest by fleeing to Switzerland, hidden in a cartload of hay. More to the point, Luxemburg was escaping to a vastly more advanced intellectual environment, where socialists from across Europe congregated and where she could pursue her scholarly studies at a level unavailable in the backward Russian Empire.

Enrolled in the University of Zurich's philosophy faculty, with a course plan heavy in mathematics and natural sciences, Luxemburg was, through her Proletariat connections, at the same time plunged into the emigré socialist movement headquartered there. In the squabbling and polemics among Zurich's Babel of grouplets, factions, and perspectives, Luxemburg was introduced to the best and the worst of the international socialist movement.

The dominant tone of both the emigré political circles centered in cities like Zurich and Paris and the established socialist parties in Germany, France, Italy, and so on was one of grinding banality. The flagship German party (the SPD) had been condemned as non-Marxist by Marx himself from before its founding in the 1860s; Wilhelm Liebknecht and August Bebel, its co-founders, had strenuously maintained and cultivated that tradition ever since. In an atmosphere of untrammelled political opportunism and profound ignorance of even the ABCs of Marxism, agentry flourished with barely any hindrance except the honest but abysmally ignorant moral commitment of the party's working-class rank and file. It is already known that Bebel and other top leaders of the party were the agents of the British Round Table financiers; the full extent of agent penetration in the SPD remains to be set out — as does the even more significant question of the degree to which Luxemburg was aware of such agent operations. Here, however, we can only sketchily indicate the political environment in which Luxemburg found herself.

A very important part of that environment was the newly formed Polish Socialist Party. The bits and pieces of the fragmented Polish movement, including organizations from all three parts of divided Poland, were pulled together into an SDS-style "unified socialist organization." The exact circumstances surrounding the creation of the PSP are unclear, but suffice it to say here that from the start its hegemonic political position was a fanatical commitment to Polish nationalism, and its wide range of backers featured the worst scum in the international social-democracy.

Nevertheless, under the PSP's all-encompassing umbrella the battle against "social patriotism" and for the working-class program continued as fervently as ever. Luxemburg, by now transfered to the University's law faculty and its political economy curriculum, was among a core of Polish intellectuals in Zurich who dragged the battle out into the open, in front of the entire social-democratic movement.

In the summer of 1893, only shortly after the PSP's founding, a Polish language newspaper titled *The Workers' Cause* (*Sprawa Robotnicza*) was brought out in Paris by Luxemburg and her circle. The paper's editorial statement of principles, written by Luxemburg, boldly declared to the hegemonic nationalists in the PSP that "the patriotic tendency, the ideal of an independent Poland, has no prospect of winning the social-democratic workers to itself." The PSP's anti-Russian propaganda was countered with the "common slogan of the united proletariat of the Russian Empire — the overthrow of absolutism," a program which "does not reckon for its realization on fortuitous transformations in European politics, does not owe its existence to the wishes and ideals of individuals and dying classes. Rather, it is bred of the objective course of history...which simultaneously develops capitalism and thereby has created the political power that will destroy it — the proletariat."

The existence of *Workers' Cause* was, Luxemburg and her comrades hoped, enough to win them a mandate to participate as an independent Polish voice in the Socialist International's Third Congress in Zurich that August, and an opportunity to take the issue before the world working class and confront not only the PSP but its patrons in the International.

When Luxemburg arrived at the conference, her mandate was immediately challenged by the PSP. Luxemburg fought back, forcing her opponents into a debate before the entire conference, with all the factitious advantage on her side. Finally, her mandate was narrowly voted down, but not before drawing fire from such big guns as Plekhanov, the patriarchal leader of the Russian movement, who angrily termed her editorial a "lying Jesuitical document." Her tendency had been launched.

Within a year, Luxemburg and her circle had built the nucleus of a new party, pointedly named the Social Democratic Party of the Kingdom of Poland (SDKP)*to make its rejection of nationalist aspirations clear. The SDKP held its first official congress in March 1894, with Luxemburg's *Workers' Cause* editorial adopted as its founding principles and the newspaper, under Luxemburg's editorial control, as its organ.

The PSP turned its considerable resources and connections to the task of destroying the aggravating new contender for leadership of the Polish movement. Accusations of police agentry were thrown at leading SDKPers, and Luxemburg and her comrades were placed in as complete isolation from the rest of the socialist movement as the PSP and its backers could enforce. But less than a year after its founding, the SDKP's success against its large, well-financed adversary was such that Luxemburg could crow in a letter to her lover and closest political collaborator, Leo Jogiches, that *Workers' Cause* "is, in the recent period, having an impact as it never did before. Because of it, the social patriots are now continually depressed, and await the appearance of each issue shaking with fear..." Sources in the Russian movement told her, she continued, that polarization within the PSP has reached such a point that her recently published pamphlet on the national question was being grabbed up by the party's members, and she had just discovered that an open factional split had surfaced in the highest levels of the PSP over the SDKP program. "In a word — *bullseye!*" she concluded. "Every blow from us hits right in the Achilles heel."

Luxemburg's concern with the "Polish question" derived only secondarily from her own roots in the Polish movement. The central issue was social-democratic policy toward the Russian empire, and here Luxemburg touched on one key to the bloody bargain between the social-democracy's leaders and the British financiers. Because these bankers were determined that Russia would provide them the greatest economic and political benefits if its economic and social backwardness were rigidly

---

* Later to become the SDKPiL.

maintained, their "left" hirelings had loyally played the other side of the same fence by always and in every way treating Russia as the unchangeable, unorganizable "bastion of reaction." To show, as Luxemburg did, that the world development of productive and political forces must necessarily reach even Mother Russia, and so provide critical leverage points to the international working-class movement, was to punch a gaping hole into the agent bell-jar which the British Round Tablers had clamped over the international social-democracy.

As a result, what many of the Second International's most powerful leaders wishfully referred to as "that Polish squabble" was becoming an international issue that soon threatened to extend the developing rift in the PSP through the heart of the social-democracy.

The heat generated within the Polish and Russian movements by the SDKP's polemics soon became great enough that toward the end of 1895 Luxemburg was able to win a hearing for her case on *Neue Zeit*, the theoretical journal of the gigantic German Social Democratic Party (SPD), as well as in its Italian counterpart. Her *Neue Zeit* article, as indicated by its title, "New Currents in the Polish Socialist Movement in Germany and Austria," drove at the "Polish question" from the standpoint of the PSP's relations to the social-democratic parties of the two other "mother countries" of divided Poland. The PSP's insistence on nationalism, she charged, had lawfully led it to contradict and even work directly against the policies and programs of the German and Austrian parties, with which it was nominally allied; by contrast the SDKP represented the principle of internationalism which must be the cornerstone of any truly socialist party.

The implications of this strike at the leaders of the German and Austrian parties were not lost on many of her readers, most particularly the controllers of the International. Beyond any of the particulars of Luxemburg's argument, the fact was that she had introduced *actual Marxism* into the social-democracy.

The full weight of authority was now applied in an attempt to silence the troublesome woman once and for all. The Russian movement's grand old man Plekhanov took up the cudgels on behalf of the PSP in a reply in *Neue Zeit*. Then, an even bigger fish, the journal's editor, Karl Kautsky, joined in with a detailed academic defense of the Polish independence demand, citing all the appropriate quotations from Marx and Engels. The choleric PSP dragged the debate into the pages of the SPD's daily newspaper, *Vorwärts*, giving Luxemburg the means to keep the question at the boiling point with counter-replies and counter-counter-replies all the way to the International's Congress in July 1896. Victor Adler, the reptilian agent who headed the Austrian Social Democratic Party, expressed the general unease among such circles in a letter to Kautsky that May. "Above all I am scared of the effect on our Daszynski (PSP leader)," Adler wrote. "*He* himself is *very* sensible, but has to deal with his — as we with our — lunatics...I implore you to send me whatever more you get in before setting it in print — not for my comments, but to enable me to calm things down, and make up for all the damage this doctrinaire goose has caused us."

But Luxemburg would not allow things to be "calmed down," even though some of her own closest collaborators were becoming thoroughly intimidated by the heavy artillery lining up against the tiny SDKP. She and her political perspectives were the talk of the International — never mind what sort of talk — and she used her new found notoreity as a càlling card to take her case to the French Socialist leaders, to every emigré Pole she could find, to the Russians, to the German social-democratic press. An indication of her success was the arrival of a conciliatory letter from the Russian Dan a few days before the conference, making an offer of cooperation on behalf of the heretofore hostile Russian organization. Wrote Luxemburg to Jogiches:

"You understand of course that this lackey is writing under orders from Plekhanov. It's clear...that Mr.P wants to make it up with us and 'permit' us to sit in the same delegation with him. And because — there are several reasons: 1. the effect of the article in *Neue Zeit*; 2. the beast sees that the social patriots' resolution (at the International Congress - TD) will flop and that ours is a protest against the Czardom. He has to vote for it, and he understands that it will be passed in this or some other form. And if that's so, then rather than stand in the side-lines and only nod his head to our active role, he'd rather take us under his wing and be the brains for every-thing...Naturally we'll turn up our noses at him."

In her reply to Dan, Luxemburg harshly told the Russians that their support of the policy and practice of the PSP, "the enemies of Polish social-democracy," precluded any collaboration.

Luxemburg arrived at this conference armed with several German mandates as well as SDKP credentials, to ensure that there could be no repetition of the 1893 difficulties. As head of the SDKP delegation, she faced off against the PSP's new leader, the super-nationalist Joseph Pilsudski (whose subsequent evolution into a full-dress fascist was to prove Luxemburg's argument in spades), and the battle over the PSP's resolution explicitly endorsing Polish independence as a primary social-democratic goal was on. Luxemburg surprised her opponents by presenting her own counter-resolution condemning national independence demand as in fundamental opposition to socialist program. In a storm of angry polemics, both resolutions were defeated in favor of the International's typical solution, a vague compromise satisfying only the "calm things down" faction, which both supported the general "right to self-determination of all nations" and affirmed the internationalist character of "the ranks of the class-conscious workers." But far more important than resolutions, Luxemburg's standing as the leading voice of an emergent Marxist left among not just the Polish and Russian movements but the entire Second International had been established with full fanfare.

Her next move was to certify her position by opening up a whole new round of debate in the social-democratic press. She turned from the "Polish question" to go directly for the throats of the Second International leadership on the issue of their stance toward the nationalist struggles which were tearing the Turkish Empire into pieces. The social-democracy, adhering to its decades-old policy of opposing whatever it seemed that Czarist absolutism favored, and vice versa — the usual argument for the Polish independence demand — had attempted to support the Turkish autocracy as a bastion against Russia, going so far as to effectively endorse Turkey's slaughter of hundreds of thousands of Armenians. That October, Luxemburg came out with a series of articles in the Dresden party newspaper, the *Sächsische Arbeiterzeitung*, in which she showed the impossibility of internally generated economic progress within backward Turkey, and therefore the inevitability of the empire's collapse into its constituent parts. It was not only a moral duty for the social-democracy to support those who "seek to free themselves from the yoke of Turkish rule," but an opportunity to use this upsurge as a weapon against the Czar's plans for the Balkans. It should not be surprising that the principled and the practical were in such accord, she tartly told the International's leaders, "since the principles and goals of the social-democracy are derived from and based on actual social development." These principles, she wrote in conclusion, were far more effective than the leadership's "attempts to pursue café politics."

The response to her latest sally was even more intense. In addition to frantic attempts to rebut her from the PSP, august, unscrupulous Wilhelm Liebknecht, still co-chairman of the SPD, took the field with an article in *Vorwärts*, giving Luxemburg the chance to raise the polemical ante even higher in a sharply worded counter-reply in the *Sächsische Arbeiterzeitung*. More clearly than ever, the point was not doctrinaire opposition to national independence in the abstract, but the ability to master the realities of the political situation — and once again Luxemburg was showing herself to be awesomely superior in that regard to the International's most respected leaders.

Now came one of the great turning points in Luxemburg's life: her decision to go beyond the relatively narrow bounds of her role in the now-thriving SDKP and take up her newly won position as an international socialist leader, by moving into the International's largest and most important party, the German SPD. It was at this point that her doctoral dissertation was written, as a final, definitive settling of accounts on the "Polish question" and a gathering of intellectual forces for what lay ahead.

We have gone into some detail about Rosa Luxemburg's political career up to this time in order to indicate what sort of woman it was who wrote *The Industrial Development of Poland*.

She had pitted her intellect and organizing abilities against, first, the leaders of the Polish movement, then those of the Russian, then of the highest levels of the International, and had found no one approaching her own mettle. Despite isolation, insults, slanders, and bitter opposition from it seemed at times all sides, she had shaped the SDKP from a handful of emigrés into a strong organization able now to begin well-organized mass work in Poland, while she personally had fought her way to a leading position in the international movement. The substantial time she now gave to researching and writing her doctorate (although admittedly not without complaint) indicates that she placed this work's value far above its immediate academic utility.

The dissertation was officially presented to the University of Zurich in the spring of 1897, and won her the title of Doctor of Law. The following year, the publishing house of Duncker and Humblot brought it out as a book, a rare honor for a social science thesis which much impressed Luxemburg's social-democratic colleagues.

In the climate she and her co-thinkers had created in the social-democracy around the Polish independence issue and its relationship to the most basic questions of revolutionary praxis, this new salvo served not only as a source of incontestable factual ammunition against the PSP, but as a carefully worked-through discussion of the *process* of capitalist development and a practical application of the quality of thinking required to grasp it. She was, indeed, using this defense of capitalism's evolutionary aspects against those who wished to turn back the historical clock as a metaphor for both the necessary development of the working-class movement and the flowering of her own intellectual powers. Her uniqueness among her contemporaries lay not simply in the "totality" of her thinking, as Lukacs and others have put it, although that aspect of her "total capitalist" rigor is immediately striking in comparison with the Robinson Crusoeisms that litter the self-styled Marxism of her adversaries. This "totality" was self-consciously a *developing* one, an actual infinity which pulled the "inner" and "outer" sides of her own existence into compelling coherence with the whole world's motion. It was the basis for the Promethean self-subsistence that enabled her to fight alone for what she knew against no matter how huge an array of opposing forces. And it gave her the power to see real social processes with precision and transparent clarity while those around her flailed about in the fog from one tactical expedient to the next.

The truth of this is clearest from the powerfully defined personality that radiates from every line of her writing, in this early work as well. Her letters from this period fix the impression even more firmly. Writing to Leo Jogiches in the spring of 1898, just after she had moved to Berlin and her new political battleground in the SPD, she described a period of deep depression as "bruises on my soul...a confused impression of disharmony...most agonizing is the feeling of incomprehension, just a hollow rushing in my head..." The opposite of this "disharmony," of this sense of loss of intellectual and thus personal identity, is the sharp-focus connectedness of intellectual work. A few days after the above letter she wrote again to Jogiches, and reproached him for his compulsive niggling over the publisher's proofs of her dissertation. Her letter is worth quoting at some length:

"Several places are, it now seems to me, pretty thin gravy, unclear," she says of her thesis, "and they should stay that way...Oh may we never have such work again! Now I hate this doctorate so, because I've put so much strength and struggle into it, that I'm seized by *crying fits* when I think of it. For these reasons I want to tell you, quite generally, the conclusions I've come to here about work methods...To do everything calmly, easily, not excite yourself even a little, not sit too long over each thing — that's my system...There are cases where work can't be spared, not even with details,...But in these cases the work *isn't* wasted: you know it in polish, in the whole and in the harmony of the form. But work like...for this doctorate is madness...When I look at the sum total of our effort and the sum of the results in the past — then I'm seized with shame. *Enough of that* — work *fresh, happy, free,* easy and joyfully, consider everything ser-iously, but *briefly;* what's already been achieved, don't mull over any further, make decisions fast and realize them fast and go, move on."

...And the Development of Capitalism in Russia

In later life, Luxemburg succeeded more and more in shaping her writing as that sort of direct, "harmonic" communication between author and audience, what, in regard to her 1913 *Anti-Kritik*, she called proudly "naked, like a block of marble." Yet certainly even in the "hated" doctorate we already see that efflorescence of ideas and jubilant mastery of creative power that was uniquely hers — especially if we compare it to a contemporary and, in certain ways, strikingly similar work by Lenin.

The same year that Luxemburg's thesis was published, Lenin was finishing a long, carefully researched, and painstakingly detailed description of the transformation which capitalism was bringing about in Russia. His book, published in 1899, was titled *The Development of Capitalism in Russia*, paralleling the title which Luxemburg unsuccessfully tried to convince her publishers to use for the book form of her thesis, *The Capitalist Development of Poland*. Lenin's polemic, like Luxemburg's, was aimed at the populist political currents which based themselves on reactionary opposition to the progressive advance of capitalism, cloaked in rhetorically Marxist anti-capitalism — in Russia, the Narodniks. "(The Narodniks) exert every effort," Lenin wrote, "to make it appear that to admit that capitalism is historically progressive means to be an apologist of capitalism." He stressed capitalism's "progressive character as compared with preceding systems of social economy...there is nothing more absurd than to conclude from the contradictions of capitalism that the latter is impossible, non-progressive, and so forth — to do that is to take refuge in the transcendental heights of romantic dreams away from unpleasant, but undoubted realities."

The differences in method and tone between the two works, however, show with painful clarity Luxemburg's towering superiority over the rest of her generation of socialist intellectuals, even its best. The sparkling ironical style of Luxemburg's doctoral thesis finds no parallel in the dry academicism of Lenin's political document. Where Luxemburg is able to paint a historical portrait of her subject, rich in telling detail (and even so felt it to be far too leaden!), Lenin begins with a catechismic recitation of contrasting quotations from his opponents, and Marx and Engels, then proceeds to pile up a Matterhorn of statistical information describing the capitalist transformation of Russia and its effect on the peasantry from every conceivable vantage point. Where Luxemburg's scope is global, Lenin's is gubernia by gubernia, factory by factory, farm by farm.

The theoretical boners which Luxemburg was later to pillory in her 1912 magnum opus *The Accumulation of Capital* appear here in abundance; in fact it was Lenin's preparatory study, *Economic Studies and Articles* (1898) that Luxemburg included in *Accumulation of Capital*'s survey of Russian Marxism. "The law of pre-capitalist modes of production is the repetition of the process of production on the previous scale," Lenin writes in his 1899 book, "on the previous basis: such are the *corvée* economy of the landlords, the natural economy of the peasants, the handicraft production of the industrialists. The law of capitalist production, on the contrary, is constant transformation of the modes of production..." As Luxemburg was to comment in *Accumulation of Capital* on Lenin's astounding failure to recognize the very existence of historical development, "It quite escapes him that under conditions of simple reproduction ("repetition on the previous scale" - TD), which he takes to be the rule for all pre-capitalist modes of production, we should probably never have advanced beyond the stage of the paleolithic scraper." (Needless to say, subsequent editions of Lenin's text have not taken advantage of Luxemburg's helpful corrective.)

Admittedly, the comparative weaknesses of Lenin's *Development of Capitalism* must to some extent be chalked up to the profound difference in his and Luxemburg's political experience at that point. Luxemburg's early history we have briefly traced. By contrast, Lenin (born only a year before Luxemburg) first appears as a political leader in 1895, when he founded the tiny League of Struggle for the Emancipation of the Working-Class, which attempted to carry on factory agitation. We get a hint of the orientation of the League's organizing from Edmund Wilson's story that Krupskaya, Lenin's future wife, "dressed like a working-class woman and visited the factory barracks" as part of her League activities. There followed long years in exile in the depths of Siberia, and it was during this time that Lenin's book was written — he did not escape to Switzerland until 1900.

His writings, decades later, reveal the same fundamental flaw, however, made all the more glaring by the importance of the issues immediately at stake. In the spring of 1914, Lenin authored a pamphlet on *The Right of Nations to Self-Determination*, in which he soars into a virtual tantrum at Luxemburg and her opposition to demands for independence from every national sector of the Russian Empire. All the clanking, wheezing machinery of the "theory of stages" is rolled out. "She *does not make the least* attempt to determine *what* historical stage in the development of capitalism *Russia* is passing through," Lenin fumes about her 1908 article, "The National Question and Autonomy." He continues, "Rosa Luxemburg refers to a pamphlet she wrote in 1898 (*The Industrial Development of Poland* - TD), proving the rapid 'industrial development of Poland,' with the latter's manufactured goods being marketed in Russia. Needless to say, no conclusion whatever can be drawn from this on the *right* to self-determination; it only proves the disappearance of the old Poland of the landed gentry, etc. But Rosa Luxemburg always passes on imperceptibly to the conclusion that among the factors that unite Russia and Poland, the purely economic factors of modern capitalist relations now predominate."

The purpose of Lenin's odd little pamphlet would be hard to make out on internal evidence alone — why so much spleen about a six-year old article? The answer lies in the ugly factional squabble which Lenin was maintaining against Luxemburg's and, particularly, Jogiches' increasing dominance in the Polish-Russian movement. In the interests of his own factional position Lenin was willing to use anything that came to hand (for example, slimy Karl Radek). While Luxemburg was in the midst of her critical battle with the leadership of the SPD over the coming world war and the very existence of the working-class movement, Lenin threw his support to the SPD leaders! Indeed, in this pamphlet he again and again holds up the wretched Kautsky as a model Marxist thinker, while he chides Luxemburg for "her inability to see things from a viewpoint any deeper and broader than that of the (Polish) anthill."

Here he fulminates about the "concrete historical particularities" of each and every section of the Russian Empire, for that seems to be the best way to achieve his immediate objective. In his *Development of Capitalism*, on the other hand, immediate tactical concerns are far different and so in this work the same problem dissolves into (as Luxemburg would put it) a "fog in which all cats are grey," almost a parody of the excesses of an untutored Luxemburg epigone: "...Where is the borderline between the home and foreign market? To take the political boundaries of the state would be too mechanical a solution...Such questions are not of great importance. What is important is that capitalism cannot exist and develop without constantly expanding...," etc.

What is revealed is no lack of either intellectual ability or (in broad terms) political morality on Lenin's part, but a pervasive cynicism about creative intellectual work itself, which harshly distinguishes the poverty of Lenin's work from the unbounded conceptual richness of Luxemburg's. This cynical "practicality" was the breeding-ground for the stifling mediocrity of Stalin, and it remains the greatest vulnerability of Lenin's heirs in the Soviet Union and the world communist movement — as their duped complicity in the suppression of Luxemburg's writings and the glorification of her most scurrilous agent-opponents indicates. The world-historic responsibilities that these forces and their international allies now immediately face makes it particularly opportune to bring Luxemburg's clear voice once again into the debate, for what is required of all of us is nothing less than the heights of intellectual courage which Rosa Luxemburg will always represent.

*   *   *

In preparing this translation, I used the text of the work's original 1898 edition as presented in Luxemburg's *Gesammelte Werke*, Vol. I-1, published in Berlin by Dietz in 1972. I have omitted Luxemburg's copious footnotes from the translation, on the assumption that the specialist to whom these detailed source references would be of interest would, in any case, consult the original German text. Metric equivalents for the Russian units of measure will be found at the end of the translation, together with a brief note on the main historical points Luxemburg touches in her discussion.

Tessa DeCarlo
December 1, 1976

THE
INDUSTRIAL
DEVELOPMENT
OF
POLAND

Dissertation for the attainment of the Doctorate of Political Science from the Political Science faculty of the University of Zurich

submitted by

ROSA LUXEMBURG
of Warsaw

Foreword

Although the subject of the following treatise is a very specialized one, we believe nonetheless that it may be of more than slight interest to the Western European reader, for several reasons. Today, economic questions stand in the forefront of the intellectual life of all civilized countries; they have already been recognized as the mainspring of all social being and becoming. The political physiognomy, the historic destiny of a country is a sealed book to us if we do not know about its economic life, with all the resulting social consequences.

It was not long ago that Poland's name echoed throughout the whole civilized world, that its fate stirred every soul and provoked excitement in every heart. Lately one no longer hears very much about Poland — since Poland is a capitalist country. Do we now want to know what became of the old rebel, where historic destiny steered it? — the answer can only be given through investigation of its economic history during the last decades. The so-called Polish question can be observed and discussed from several standpoints, but for those who recognize that the material development of a society is the key to its political development, the Polish question can only be solved on the basis of Poland's economic life and its tendencies. We have endeavored to collect the existing material for the solution of the problem in the following discussion, and to arrange it as clearly as possible, at the same time permitting ourselves some direct observations of a political nature here and there. So this topic, which at first glance might appear dry and specialized, may be of some interest to the politician as well.

But for still other reasons. We live in a time when the powerful Empire of the North plays an ever more important role in European politics. All eyes are turned persistently toward Russia, and the alarming progress of Russian policy in Asia is watched with apprehension. Probably it will soon be a secret to no one that even the most important capitalist countries must prepare themselves for a serious *economic* rivalry with Russia in Asia sooner or later. Therefore, the economic policy of the Czarist empire surely cannot be a matter of complete indifference to Western Europeans. Poland, however, constitutes one of the most important and most progressive industrial districts of the Russian Empire, in fact one in whose history the economic policy of Russia finds perhaps its clearest expression.

The material for our work lay strewn in countless and, in many cases, contradictory statistical works, polemical brochures, newspaper articles, official and unofficial reports; a thorough study of the history of Polish industry as a whole, and in particular of its present position, is to be found in neither the Polish nor the Russian or German literature. Accordingly, we believed that this raw and fragmentary material had to be digested and presented in the most finished possible form, in order to bring the reader to general conclusions as smoothly as possible.

Part 1

The History
and Present State
of Polish Industry

1.1 The Manufacturing Period, 1820-1850

Political events moved Poland into a completely new situation at the beginning of the nineteenth century. The partition brought it out of the peculiar natural-economic, feudal-anarchic conditions of the republic of the nobles which we find in the Poland of the eighteenth century, and placed it under the rule of enlightened absolutism and under the centralized bureaucratic administration of Prussia, Austria, and Russia.* The Russian section of Poland, which interests us here, admittedly maintained its own corporative constitution while still the Duchy of Warsaw and later after the Vienna Congress. But it was as different from the old Poland as heaven from earth, and the whole administrative, financial, military, legal government apparatus was tailored to a modern centralized state. The latter found itself in the harshest contradiction with the economic relations on which it had been grafted.

---

* see Appendix

THE INDUSTRIAL DEVELOPMENT OF POLAND

Poland's economic life, as before, was concentrated on land ownership. The development of urban handicraft begun in the thirteenth century had crumbled to dust by the seventeenth century; the attempt by the magnates to start up manufacturing at the end of the eighteenth century disintegrated likewise. The system of land ownership, however, was utterly unsuited to serve as the basis of a modern state organization. Its dependence on the world market, which dated from the fifteenth century in old Poland, drove it to an extremely extensive latifundia economy and the utmost exaction of forced labor; it became more and more irrationally cultivated and as a result more and more unproductive. The wars during Poland's last epoch, then the Napoleonic system in the Duchy of Warsaw, the continental blockade and with it the decline of grain exports, the drop in grain prices, the abolition of serfdom in 1807,* all these blows rained down on landed property in the course of approximately ten years and brought it to the brink of ruin. Since it was, meanwhile, the main source of revenue in the country, the relatively high cost of the country's new administration had to fall on it full force. The ten per cent income tax on landed property, already introduced in old Poland but only now actually collected, was now to be raised to 24 per cent. The burden of quartering soldiers and providing supplies for the military *in natura* fell on the nobility in addition.

The result was that landed property soon fell into the clutches of usury. While old Poland possessed no urban capitalist class, as a result of the decay of urban production and trade, such a class surfaced right after the partition of Poland. In part it consisted of immigrating officials and usurers, in part of Polish parvenues who owed their material existence to the country's great political and economic crisis. This new layer of the population now supplied the needy nobility with capital. To a large extent, however, the beginning of the nobility's indebtedness dated from the ten years of Prussian rule (1796-1806), during which an organized agricultural credit was widely offered to the Polish nobility for the first time.

For Polish landed property this meant a real revolution. What was accomplished in Western European countries during the Middle Ages through a slow and persistent process over

---

* see Appendix

centuries—the disintegration of patrimonial land ownership through usury—was now achieved in Poland, where landed property had kept itself free from usury until the end of the Republic, in less than 20 years. Already in the year 1821 it had to be rescued from downfall by the government of the Kingdom by means of an exceptional measure—the moratorium.

Under such circumstances, the deficit became a permanent phenomenon in the Kingdom's budget right from the beginning. The creation of new sources of revenue for the exchequer and of new spheres of economic activity in the country therefore became a condition of existence for the Kingdom from the first moment. Following the example of other countries and driven by immediate needs, the government undertook the establishment of urban industry in Poland.

The decade 1820-1830 is the period of the rise of Polish industry, or, more correctly, of Polish manufacture.

It was quite similar in character to the earlier rise of Polish handicraft by the method of attracting foreign, mainly German craftsmen. Just as in the thirteenth century the Polish princes tried to entice foreign workers to Poland with a variety of privileges, so also the government of Congress Poland. A whole series of Czarist ukases relating to this were proclaimed in the years 1816 to 1824. The government provided houses and made building materials available gratis, gave rent exemptions, founded the so-called iron fund for the construction of industrial buildings and housing for industry. In 1816, immigrating craftsmen were promised freedom from all taxes and public charges for six years, their sons were freed from military service, and the duty-free import of their property was permitted. In 1820, the government granted the immigrants a free supply of building materials from the state forests and constructed its own brickyards in order to supply them with the cheapest possible bricks.

A law of the year 1822 freed all industrial enterprises from the obligation to quarter soldiers for three to six years. In 1820 and 1823, it was decreed that the cities were to hand over locations to these enterprises rent-free for six years. The industrial fund established in 1822 for the encouragement of industrial colonization amounted to 45,000 rubles at the beginning, already twice as much in 1823, and from then on 127,500 rubles annually.

THE INDUSTRIAL DEVELOPMENT OF POLAND

Such manifold attractions did not fail to have an effect. Soon German craftsmen trooped into Poland and settled down. Approximately 10,000 German families immigrated in a few years at this time. In this way, the most important industrial cities of today soon arose: Lodz, Zgierz, Rawa, Pabianice, and others. In addition to craftsmen, the government of Russian Poland called in prominent foreign industrialists to direct its enterprises: Coqueril from Belgium, Fraget, Girard, and others. Russian Poland's government did not content itself with the granting of privileges to immigrants and the establishment of German manufacturing towns, however. Unlike the handicrafts of the Middle Ages, manufacturing could not content itself with the narrow circle of consumption and circulation within any one city; to start with, it required a wholesale market and, further, commodity circulation embracing the whole country at least. Together with the foundation of manufacturing colonies, the government had to undertake a whole series of administrative and legislative reforms which were to unify the country economically into one complex and create the necessary legal forms for internal commodity traffic. The greatest breach in the property relations and especially the landed property relations of old Poland had already been forced by the the Code Napoleon introduced in the Duchy of Warsaw in 1808. It had grafted the legal forms of a modern bourgeois economy in quite finished form onto the economic conditions of a purely feudal natural economy. Unable to reorganize the means of production as such in the slightest, it had nevertheless severely violated the old property relations and so hurried their disintegration. With the abolition of perpetual rent, entail, etc., landed property was torn out of permanence and catapulted into circulation. At the same time, the Code Napoleon supplied commerce and the commercial courts with legal standards. In 1817, furthermore, chambers of commerce and manufacturing were established and the regulation of trade was brought to a close; in the following year, deed registries were introduced; in 1825, the Agricultural Credit Association was founded. In 1819, the building of highways and the regulation of waterways was begun by order of the state, and in 1825, the construction of the canal between the Njemen and the Vistula.

Finally, the government also took the lead—as in other countries at the beginnings of manufacture—with its own industrial enterprises, and established model factories, model sheep-raising, and so on. But it gave the strongest foothold to budding manufacturing by establishing the Polish Bank, which was called into existence by the Czarist ukase of 1828 and organized after the model of the German *Seehandlung* and the Belgian *Société générale.* This was an issuing, investment, deposit, mortgage, commission, and industrial bank all at once. Initially endowed with a fund amounting to 3 million rubles, it also obtained deposits, securities, ecclesiastical funds, fire insurance, pensions, and other capitals on deposit, which by 1877 represented 282 million rubles total. The bank offered credit to industry as well as to agriculture. In the period of 50 years since its founding, it had given commercial and industrial enterprises alone credit to the amount of 91 million rubles. The activity of the bank was extremely diverse. It not only established factories itself and carried on mining and agriculture, but also attended to means of transport. The first Polish train line, Warsaw-Vienna, of 1845 was chiefly the work of the Polish Bank.

The activity of the government sketched above was the first important factor in the development of industry in Russian Poland. Whatever other circumstances may have additionally influenced its history, it unquestionably owes its existence to the initiative and efforts of the government.

We see of course—as was said—that in other countries, for example France and Germany, governments stand by the cradle of manufacturing and take hold of its destiny with energetic hands. But there the governments offered their help only to a natural development of urban production, which moved of itself and by virtue of objective factors such as the accumulation of trading capital, the widening of markets, and the technological development of handicraft toward transformation into manufacturing production methods. In Poland, manufacture, like urban handicraft earlier, was a foreign product imported in finished form, which could develop neither a technological nor a social connection to Poland's own economic development. Here, then, the activity of the government was the only positive factor in the rise of manufacture, and this explains to us the predilection which Polish economists and publicists have for reverting to this point; thus its significance is on the whole only too often overestimated. Above all, they forget that the autonomous Polish government, in the activity that they describe, acted in the most intimate agreement with Russian Czarism, which was guided by intentions which were in national terms nothing less than friendly toward Poland.

Furthermore, from the first, the assistance of Russian Poland's government fell on the most favorable soil: Poland's tariff relations. The Vienna Congress Act resulted in two important measures for Poland in this connection: First, it was united with Russia. Second, free trade with the other sections of what was formerly Poland, or what in fact meant the same thing, with Germany and Austria, was secured. As far as the union with Russia is concerned, the trade relations between the two countries were regulated by the tariffs of 1822 and 1824 so that their products were exchanged with each other almost duty-free.

The meaning of this new regulation for Poland only becomes clear, however, if it is kept in mind that since the year 1810, and especially under the administration of Kankrin, Russia adhered to an extreme prohibitive policy toward Europe, often bordering on absurdity, and was protected on all sides from foreign manufacture by an unbreachable tariff wall. Through the unification with Poland, Russia was now made accessible to German goods from this side, because of the above-mentioned tariff. The result of this for Poland was that it became the workshop for the processing of half-finished German goods, most of which were imported into Russian Poland duty-free, finished in Poland, and which then found their way into Russia as Polish products, again almost duty-free. By such means Poland's large cloth industry, in particular, came into full bloom in only a few years.

First established in the years 1817 to 1826, it had already, in 1829, reached the, for that time, considerable amount of 5,752,000 rubles' worth of production. That this surprisingly rapid growth was almost entirely thanks to Russian consumption is shown by the following table of exports of wool products to Russia, in thousands of rubles:

1823:	1,865
1825:	5,058
1827:	7,218
1829:	8,418.

THE INDUSTRIAL DEVELOPMENT OF POLAND

If the value of exported products according to this table exceeds the value of that produced in the country, this is because of the fact that, along with goods finished in Poland, German finished products smuggled into Poland were massively exported to Russia under Polish labels.

But this tariff relationship had still another important side for Congress Poland. It opened to her a free trade route to China, where Polish cloth was likewise exported in large quantities. This export specifically amounted to (in thousands of rubles):

1824:	331
1826:	332
1828:	1,024
1830:	1,070

Although Poland's whole export trade in the first decade of its industrial development really extended to only one branch, the wool industry, yet its importance for the country was great, for it also had invigorating repercussions on other branches of production and strongly encouraged the immigration of German craftsmen. A historian of the Polish textile industry center, the city of Lodz, calls Poland's cloth trade of that time with Russia and China "the mainspring of the development of industry."

Yet, in 1831, this trade came to an end. The Polish uprising,* which paralyzed the development of manufacture in the country for some time, in addition had as a lasting effect that in this year the tariff between Poland and Russia was significantly increased. The competition of Polish cloth in Russia and China had been a thorn in the side of Russian manufacturers for a long time. Their repeated petitions to increase tariffs at the Polish border remained unsuccessful, however, until the uprising of 1831 and with it the standstill of Polish cloth exports to Russia. This furnished the Russian manufacturers with the opportunity to quickly take the deserted field by expanding their own production and so prove to the government with figures how much the "Fatherland's" industry had suffered from Polish competition until then. With the raising of the tariff and, at the same time, the abolition of free transit to China, Polish exports sank rapidly:

---

* see Appendix

In 1834, they amounted to	
a total of	2,887,000 rubles,
of that manufactured products	2,385,000 rubles,
In 1850, they amounted to	
a total of	1,274,000 rubles,
of that manufactured products	755,000 rubles.

For Polish wool production, this was a hard blow. After its value had reached, in 1829—as we saw—the height of 5,752,000 rubles, it sank in 1832 to 1,917,000 and rose only little by little to 2,564,000 rubles in 1850, that is, to half of the earlier amount.

Yet, the closing of the Russian border could have no great significance for the further destiny of Polish manufacturing as a whole. The conditions for a growing demand for manufactured goods did not then exist in Russia itself, nor were the means of transport adapted to mass transport. The large cloth export trade can be explained in the main only by the needs of the Russian Army. Moreover, Polish manufacturing had still not even had time to provide itself with an internal market. So, after the closing of the Russian customs border, it slowly set out to get a foothold within the country, with favorable government measures and supported in particular by the Polish Bank. In the next two decades, many branches of production developed well: in the 1830s, tanning and soap-making, in the 1840s, sugar production, also mining in the 1830s and similarly paper manufacturing. But the country's social situation drew rather narrow bounds for the growth of industry. Totaling only the tiny number of 4 to 5 million people, the population of Russian Poland moreover lived in large part within a natural economy. Despite the abolition of serfdom in 1807,* forced labor remained the predominant mode of labor in agriculture and as a result the property owners, just as the peasants, were cut off from commodity and money exchange to a great degree. The cities grew only slowly and, poor and underpopulated as they were, could not provide a strong demand for manufactured goods either. This development is thus really a very slow one. Thirty years after Polish manufacture arose, after a period in which it had been mainly directed toward its own internal market, we see that it is still restricted to quite dwarfish dimensions. The most

---

* see Appendix

advanced of all industries, textiles, was still mainly run with manual labor in the 1850s, without steam power, and therefore only by skilled master craftsmen and journeymen and without a trace of female labor. On the whole the fragmentation of production points to its predominantly craft character, for in the year 1857 we still see 12,542 "factories" in Poland with 56,364 workers and 21,278,592 rubles' worth of production: on the average, four to five workers and 1,700 rubles' worth of production per "factory."

Corresponding to this situation, urban industry also played only a secondary role in Poland's social life until the 1850s and even the 1860s. Landed property still set the tone in the economy as well as the politics of the country. Indeed the broad mass of the middle landowners, those who at the time represented public opinion, regarded the budding urban industry and with it the capitalist economy as a foreign and poisonous weed, as a "German swindle," which bore the guilt for the desperate condition of landed property and of the whole country.

1.2 The Transition to Large-Scale Industry, 1850-1870

We have become acquainted with the first beginnings and development of industry in Poland within the internal market. We have seen that it owes its start to the efforts of the government, and that as a result of the limited internal market it was not able to divest itself of the manufacturing form even into the 1850s. But here the first epoch of its history ends, and a new page begins. Beginning in the 1850s, a series of new circumstances arose which, although in themselves very diverse, ultimately had the effect that the Russian market was opened up to Polish production, which was thus assured a mass market. This gradually brought about a complete revolution in Polish industry and transformed it from manufacture into genuine mass-production, large-scale industry. Therefore, we can characterize the second period of its history as the period of large-scale industry. The decades 1850-1870 constitute the transition period from the first to the second phase.

THE INDUSTRIAL DEVELOPMENT OF POLAND

There were four important factors which revolutionized Polish industry in this period.

First, the abolition of the customs-barrier between Russia and Poland. In the year 1851, Poland's tariff relations were remodeled in two ways. On the one hand, the tariff which until then had cut Poland off from Russia was set aside, on the other, an end was made of Poland's independent policy on trade coming in from outside, and Poland was admitted into the Russian tariff zone. In this way, Poland has formed a single whole with Russia in reference to trade ever since. For Poland, the great significance of the tariff reform of 1851 lay first of all in the fact that completely free export trade to Russia was now possible. So Polish manufacture had the prospect of producing for a mass market, of overstepping the narrow limits of the domestic market and becoming real mass-production industry. However, this result could only take effect after a long period of time. At the moment when the tariff barrier between Poland and Russia was set aside, three important hindrances still stood in the way of a real mass export of Polish manufactures to Russia. First, since it had until then been adjusted mainly to the demands of the domestic market, manufacture in Poland was still not capable of the rapid expansion by leaps and bounds which characterizes large-scale mass-production industry to such a great extent. Second, no modern means of transport existed between Poland and Russia; third, the domestic market in Russia was also of limited dimensions, restricted by the persistence of serfdom and of natural economy. But soon a complete transformation occurred in all three areas.

Certainly the *Crimean War* had a revolutionizing effect on Polish as well as on Russian manufacturing. The blockade of Russia's sea borders cut off the import of foreign goods for the most part, and the rest were redirected to the western land borders, to Poland, which became the route of lively trade traffic. But more important was the mass demand created by the needs of the Russian army, above all for products of the textile industry. In Russia, the growth of the latter in the years 1856-1860 amounted to 11.6 per cent yearly for cotton spinning, 5.5 per cent for cotton weaving, and 9.4 per cent for dyeing and finishing. In Poland, an even greater jump is observable. The value of production in thousands of rubles was:

	1854	1860	+%
in the linen industry	723	1,247	+72%
in the wool industry	2,044	4,354	+113%
in the cotton industry	2,853	8,091	+183%

The Crimean War period gave rise to a profound transformation in the technology of the textile industry as well: it brought about the introduction of the mechanical loom and the mechanical spindle in Russia and Poland. First, the now-gigantic Scheibler factory was founded in Lodz in 1854, with 100 looms and 18,000 spindles. The following year, the first mechanical linen spinning mill was established in Russia, and in 1857, the biggest and today still important linen factory in Poland, the Zyradow factory, was converted from a hand to a mechanical weaving mill.

The *second* important result was the establishment of a *series of railway lines* between Poland and the most distant parts of Russia. In 1862, Poland was connected with St. Petersburg, in 1866 with Wolynien, White Russia, and Podolien, in 1870 with Moscow, in 1871 with Kiev, in 1877 with southern Russia. Moreover, with the feverish building of railway lines in inner Russia ever more areas were opened to trade. The construction of each new railway line leading to Russia was followed by an increase in demand for Polish products and an expansion of production. Disregarding the depressive effects of the uprising of 1864 and the consequent temporary paralysis of trade with Russia, the decade 1860-1870, the period of the technological revolution in transport, had as a result that while the total value of Poland's industrial production amounted to only 31 million rubles in 1851 (21 million, according to another source), it represented 73 million rubles (from both sources) in 1872, after 15 years—an increase of 135 per cent and 248 per cent respectively.

The *third factor* which contributed to the industrial revolution was the *abolition of serfdom* in Russia in 1861 and in Poland in 1864* and the resulting transformation of agriculture. Now robbed of the unpaid labor power of the villeins, the landowners turned to the employment of wage laborers and the purchase of industrial products which earlier they had made on

---

* see Appendix

their own estates. On the other side, the great mass of peasants consequently had money to spend, and also became buyers of factory goods. Connected with this was a tax reform and the beginning of the government's policy of squeezing the Russian peasantry, which violently pushed even the small peasant onto the market with the products of his labor and, as it undermined the agricultural natural economy more and more, to that degree prepared the ground for a money economy and the mass market for manufactured goods. The other result of the reform was the proletarianization of broad layers of the peasantry, thus the "setting free" of a mass of workers who put themselves at industry's disposal.

So in Russia, we see a transformation of all social relations in connection with the Crimean War. The collapse of the old patrimonial land ownership and of natural economy, the reformation of taxation and finance, the establishment of a whole network of railways—all this meant the creation of markets, market channels, and workers for Russian industry. But since, in terms of trade policy, Poland formed a single whole with Russia ever since the tariff abolition of 1851, so Polish manufacture was swept into the whirlpool of Russia's economic metamorphosis and was transformed by the rapidly growing market into real mass-production industry.

But at the end of the 1870s yet *a fourth important factor* supervened, which within a few years made Polish industrial production into large-scale industry, such as we see today in Poland, and this is *Russia's tariff policy.*

1.3 The Period of Large-Scale Industry in Poland

Since the beginning of the century, Russia, as was mentioned, adhered to a highly protectionist policy. The Crimean War, however, caused a change here as in all other areas of social life. In the "liberal period" of the 1860s tariffs were significantly reduced. This free-trade turn did not last long, however. Because of the reforms themselves, especially the costly railroad construction, the government ran enormously into debt to foreign countries, and the gold tariff was introduced in 1877 with the object of getting hold of gold. With this, Russia entered onto a course of even stricter protectionist policies.

With the exchange rate of the paper ruble falling, the gold tariff meant an increase in the tariff rate of 30 per cent the first years and of 40 to 50 per cent in following years. In 1880, a deficit in the state treasury developed once more as a result of the abolition of the salt tax. A general tariff increase of 10 per cent ensued in 1881 as a replacement. In 1882, several individual tariff rates were raised, such as those for linen, wool yarn, chemical products, dyes, etc.; in 1884, a repeated increase in various individual tariff rates occurred, for example that for silk yarn; in 1885, an almost general increase of the tariff of 20 per cent; in 1887, once again a partial climb in individual tariffs, and the same in 1891.

Obviously the purpose of protectionism when not fiscal revenue was *above all* protection of domestic industry from foreign competition.

The results of such a substantial forcing up of the tariff were two-fold. First, the import of foreign manufactured and half-finished goods declined rapidly. The total imports over Russia's European borders in millions of gold rubles annually amounted to:

1851-56	74	1876-81	326
1856-61	120	1881-86	304
1861-66	121	1886-91	224
1866-71	212	1891	220
1871-76	364	1892	219

The import of manufactured and half-finished goods, which were dutied much higher than raw materials, shriveled up even more severely than the above table indicates. Thus a place was made in Russian markets for native — Russian and Polish — industry, which was freed to a great extent from foreign competition.

The other natural result was the general climb in commodity prices. It has recently been calculated that the Russian consumer may pay much more for most commodities than, e.g., the German consumer; thus

for tea	304%
for tobacco	687%
for coal	200%
for paper	690%
for linen	225%
for cotton products	357%
for agricultural machinery	159%

As for the metal industry: a pood of wire nails of medium size, for example, costs an American 1 to 1.50 rubles, while a Russian pays 3.20 rubles in tariffs alone on these articles and 4 to

8 rubles for the whole product. In relation to the value of the most important metals, the tariff in 1896 made up: iron ore, 70 per cent; iron, 45 per cent; and steel, 35 per cent.

Under such monopoly conditions Russian and Polish industry began to rake in colossal profits from the domestic market. We can get an approximate notion of these profits from the official statements of the manufacturers themselves. In 1887, for example, net profits were declared:

by the Russian Cotton Spinning Mills, St. Petersburg	15.0%
by the Moscow Manufacturing Company	16.0%
by the Balin Manufacturing Company	16.0%
by the Narva Linen Spinning Mill	18.0%
by the Sampson Cotton Spinning Mill	21.3%
by the Yekaterinhof Cotton Spinning Mill	23.0%
Rabeneck Cotton Dye Works	25.4%
by the Izmailov Cotton Spinning Mill	26.0%
by the S. Morosov Works	28.0%
Neva Cotton Weaving Mill	38.0%
by the Krenholm Works	44.9%
by the Thornton Wool Works	45.0%

From more recent times we have no less surprising statements of profits in the Russian metal industry. The metalurgical enterprises of the southern district yield *on the average* a profit of 50 per cent, the colossal works of the Englishman Hughes as much as 100 per cent. "Not without interest," writes the Ministry of France's official organ, "is the utilization of the profits obtained, which gives rise to the impression that the companies, faced with a downright excess of profits, are as it were uncertain what to do with them," i.e., under which column in the official reports to enter the winnings so as to conceal their staggering size.

The influence of monopoly prices on the size of capitalist profits, together with the relationship of the latter to outlays for labor power, is most strikingly shown by the following little juxtaposition. The market price of raw iron in Kiev in July, 1897, amounted to 85 kopeks per pood; of that the costs of production in Russia made up 45 kopeks, including wages at 4 kopeks per pood — with a net profit of 40 kopeks. The relation of profits to cost of production and to wages was thus 10:11 and 10:1 respectively.

The profits of Polish entrepreneurs were in no way inferior to the enormous profits of the Russians, as we will see. For example, at the beginning of the 1890s, the dividends of the sugar factories in Poland amounted to as much as 29 per cent. In the textile industry, 40 per cent profits were regarded as a normal phenomenon. But these official manufacturers' statements are notoriously 30 to 50 per cent smaller than the profits actually obtained.

Thus, after all the main conditions of industrial development — a domestic market, means of transport, an industrial reserve army — had been called to life in the years 1860-1877, the supervening tariff policy created a hot-house atmosphere of monopoly prices, which placed Russian and Polish industry in an absolute El Dorado of primitive capitalist accumulation. In the year 1877, an era of feverish enterprise and grandiose accumulation of capital began, combined with the bounding growth of production. The total picture of Poland's industrial development under the effect of the relationships sketched above shows itself as follows:

| | In millions of rubles | | | |
	Total Production	Cotton Industry	Wool Industry	Linen Industry
1860	50.0 (1864)	8.1	4.3	1.2
1870	63.9	10.2	4.0	1.2
1880	171.8	33.0	22.0	5.0
1890	240.0	47.6 (1891)	35.5	6.5

The strongest upswing between 1870 and 1880 — for all industry +169 per cent, for the cotton industry +223 per cent, for the wool industry +450 per cent, for the linen industry +317 per cent — is chiefly a result of the first three years (1877-80) of the new era in tariff policy. As we will see below, the introduction of the gold tariff brought with it not only the sudden establishment of many new enterprises but also the transfer of a number of German factories from Saxony and Silesia to the western part of Poland.

Of the largest factories which the official inquiry organized in 1886 found in Poland,

18.1%	were founded before 1850,
6.8%	in 1850-60
13.6%	in 1860-70
29.0%	in 1870-80
32.5%	in 1880-86;

thus 61 per cent of all large factories were established after 1870. As for the extent of production, in the period 1870-1890 it had almost sextupled in the textile industry as a whole. The following table shows quite specifically the influence of the tariff policy: of the most significant factories,

18.1%	were founded before 1850,
37.2%	in 1850-1877
44.7%	in 1877-1886.

Thus almost half (today even more) of all the large factories in Poland originated since 1877 as direct results of the protectionist tariff policy.

This expansion of production went hand-in-hand with a revolution in the means of production themselves. Everywhere in place of the small, scattered factories appeared modern industrial large-scale enterprises with extensive use of steam power and the newest technical equipment in construction and operation. The concentration in industry in general in Poland presents itself as follows:

	1871	1880	1890
Number of workers	76,616	120,763	ca.150,000
Value of production (in million rubles)	66.7	171.8	240
For one firm (in rubles)	3,239	8,063	71,248
For one worker (in rubles)	882	1,422	1,600

However here the average figures are, as usual, not suited to giving a true idea of the revolution taking place, since this was of course not accomplished equally in all branches of industry. Most characteristic are the figures for the *textile industry*. Here we find:

	1871	1880	1890
Number of factories	11,227	10,871	635
Number of workers	28,046	45,753	60,288
Production (in million rubles)	18.1	57.6	88.4
Workers per factory	2.5	4.2	95
Production per factory (in rubles)	1,612	5,303	139,298

But within the textile industry the *cotton industry* shows the revolution in the most vivid way:

	1871	1880	1891
Number of factories	10,499	3,881	163
Number of workers	19,894	19,576	26,307
Production (in million rubles)	10.4	30.8	47.6
Workers per factory	1.9	5	162
Production per factory (in rubles)	994	7,950	291,736

The surprising growth of the cotton industry can also be measured in the number of spindles. These amount to:

1836	7,300
1840	27,300
1850	61,300
1863	116,200
1870	289,500
1875	385,500
1879	449,600
1882	467,600
1888	ca.600,000

According to other sources the number of spindles grew during a period of ten years (1877-1886) from 216,640 to 505,622, i.e., 134 per cent. In the same period, the number of spindles in the Russian cotton industry shows an increase of 32 per cent (in particular, 45 per cent in the Moscow district, 10 per cent in the Petersburg district); that in the North American industry (1881-1891) 30 per cent, and in the English 8 per cent. The number of looms grew from 1877 to 1886: in the Russian cotton industry 46 per cent (in particular, 50 per cent in the Moscow district, 25 per cent in the Petersburg district), but in Poland 139 per cent.

The use of steam power to a greater extent begins only in the 1870s, but since then it has grown quickly.

	1875	1890
Steam horsepower in industry as a whole	14,657	51,800
of that:		
in the textile industry	4,220	26,772
in mining	1,803	10,497

In the branches on which an excise was not levied, steam horsepower almost doubled again in the two-year period from 1890 to 1892, growing from 41,303 to 81,346.

In 25 years, the whole outward appearance of the country had changed from the ground up. In the midst of this, the little town of *Lodz* quickly grew up into a large center of the textile industry, into a "Polish Manchester," with the typical appearance of a modern factory city — countless smoking factory chimneys packed tightly one next to the other, a population made up almost exclusively of factory personnel, and a municipal life regulated by factory whistles, revolving exclusively around industry and trade. Here we find a series of giant establishments, among which the Scheibler factory with its yearly production of 15 million and its 7,000 workers claims first place. In the south-western corner of the country, on the Prussian border, a whole new industrial area sprang up as though charmed out of the ground, where factories suddenly emerged amid forests and rivers, preceding the building of cities, with everything grouped around them from the beginning. In the old capital, Warsaw, the collection point for all handicrafts, handicraft greatly elevated itself. But at the same time it frequently fell under the domination of merchants' capital. Small- and middle-sized independent workshops dissolved themselves into cottage industry, and large warehouses of finished handcrafted goods stepped into the foreground as collection points for small production. The trade of the whole country was concentrated from now on in the Stock Exchange and in countless banking and commission firms.

Praga, a suburb of Warsaw, became the center of large-scale metal industry and the gigantic Zyrardow linen factory in Warsaw with its 8,000 workers transformed itself into its own little city.

1.4 Poland's Main
Industrial Districts

Now that we have given a general summary of the development of Polish industry, it remains for us to illustrate this in detail in the individual histories of the most important branches of industry, and to sketch the outward local grouping of factory production.

If we disregard the scattered, insignificant factories to the right of the Vistula and along the Prussian border, the industry of the Kingdom of Poland is concentrated in three districts with strongly stamped physiognomies, different characters, and different histories.

The most important among them is the *Lodz district*. It includes the city of Lodz and its region, further the cities of Pabianice, Tomaszow, and some districts of the Kalisch gubernia. The production of this district amounted to 49 million rubles in 1885, and today at least 120 million. This is the real *textile industry district*. Its main center, *Lodz*, is in its history extremely typical for all of Polish industry.

THE INDUSTRIAL DEVELOPMENT OF POLAND

It would be difficult to imagine a less favorable place for the founding of an industrial city than Lodz. It lies in a treeless, waterless plain, in the midst of bogs, which only about ten years ago lay on both sides of the main street here and there, so that in these places the city was barely 200 paces wide. The tiny Lodka River is completely fouled by factory waste, and all necessary water comes to the factories from artesian wells and ponds. In the year 1821, Lodz had only 112 houses with 800 inhabitants. But in 1823 colonization began, Silesian and Saxon clothmakers settled down, and by 1827 Lodz counted 2,840 inhabitants, among them 322 manufacturing workers. In 1837 it had more than 10,000, in 1840 18,600 inhabitants and over 1.1 million rubles' production annually.

As a result of the increase of the Russian customs tariff in 1831, however, and the crisis which therefore occurred in cloth-making, the growth of the city was curbed, and the number of inhabitants even declined in 1850 to 15,600. But since the 1860s, as a result of the causes described above which all together amounted to the opening up of the Russian market, there begins for Lodz an epoch of rapid development, which has become torrential since the 1870s. For in Lodz we see:

1860	32,000 inhabitants	and	2,600,000 rubles' production
1878	100,000 inhabitants	and	26,000,000 rubles' production
1885	150,000 inhabitants	and	36,500,000 rubles' production
1895	315,000 inhabitants	and	90,000,000 rubles' production

In the last 25 years, production in Lodz was also transformed. Up until the 1870s, cotton goods were made for a limited market, primarily for the well-to-do classes. But when the Russian market was opened to Polish industry and gradually a new class of customers, the working population, began to play the leading role in demand, the textile industry in Lodz had to adjust itself to the new customers. So the Lodz factories went over to the production of cheaper and simpler cotton goods, such as tricot and other crudely printed material, but above all to the production of fustian. Fabrication of this cloth was first transplanted from Saxony to the city of Pabianice in 1873. Today it dominates the entire production of the district, as the following figures show. In Lodz was manufactured:

	1881	1886
Lancort	29 %	27%
Bjas	44 %	29%
Fustian	10 %	35%
Mitkal	5.5%	5%
Miscellaneous	11.5%	4%
	100 %	100%

The sudden turn in the tariff policy in 1877 also called to life a new branch of the cotton industry in the Lodz district, namely the fabrication of so-called mixed yarn from cotton and wool (vignone). Until that time massively imported to Russia from Werdau and Crimmitschau, this product found its entry into Russia closed shortly after the introduction of the gold tariff. To circumvent this tariff wall, several factories were now transferred directly from Saxony to Lodz by German entrepreneurs, and by 1886 over 39,000 spindles of mixed yarn were manufactured here.

In this way the current configuration of the large cotton industry in the Lodz district appears as a product of the opening of the Russian market and of Russian customs policy in the 1870s.

The district's wool industry is dominated no less by the same factors. The powerful jump in production from 4 millions in 1870 to 22 millions in 1880 shows what influence the Russian market exerted on this Polish industrial branch. As for wool spinning in particular, it owes its current development quite particularly to Russia's customs policy. The introduction of the gold tariff in 1877 had the transplantation of many foreign spinning mills to Lodz as an immediate consequence; the largest, with 22,000 spindles, was founded in 1879 by Allart Rousseau Fils and is today still an affiliate of this firm in Roubaix, where it also obtains its half-finished goods. Since the 1870s, Poland became the source of supply of yarn for Russia, and its production in this branch surpasses the Russian by more than 217 per cent; in Poland it amounted to 18,749,000 rubles in 1890, in Russia 5,909,000 rubles. In the most recent periods, the customs policy has helped two other branches of the textile industry in Lodz — stocking and knitting mills — to blossom.

A still more interesting illustration of the effect of Russian customs policy on Polish industry is offered by the history of the *second district — Sosnowiec.*

This includes the southwestern part of the Piotrkov gubernia, lying close to the Prussian border, with the cities of Czestochova, Bedzin, Zaviercie, Sielce, and Sosnowiec. While the Lodz district began its industrial development in the 1820s, the industry of the Sosnowiec district, as was mentioned, represents a phenomenon of quite recent date.

Up until the 1860s, there was nothing to be seen here but miles of thick pine forests, but within 15 years this forest region transformed itself into a lively industrial area, whose textile industry is already beginning to give serious competition to that of old Lodz.

There were two important circumstances which greatly favored the rapid development of industry in the Sosnowiec district. First, the cheapness of fuel. The southern part of the Piotrkov gubernia forms the coal basin of Poland, and its nearness put young Sosnowiec industry in an outstandingly advantageous position in comparison with not only Russia but also the other parts of Poland. The average price of one pood of coal in the districts concerned, by place, amounts to:

Sosnowiec district	2.40 - 9.7 kopeks
Warsaw district	11.22 - 13.0 kopeks
Lodz district	11.50 - 14.9 kopeks

Second, the cheapness of labor. From the outset, this coal industry placed a contingent of "free" female labor power at the disposal of the factories of the district, in the persons of the members of the miners' families. Here too the Sosnowiec district finds itself in a significantly more advantageous position than the Lodz district. Specifically, wages per month in rubles amount to:

	Sosnowiec District			Lodz District		
	Men	Women	Children	Men	Women	Children
Finishing	13.50	10.75	8.50	26.00	18.0	9.75
Wool spinning	29.25	9.0	6.0	28.25	18.25	6.0
Mixed spinning	21.25	10.25	—	22.0	13.0	—
Cotton spinning	15.75	11.0	4.75	21.0	17.75	4.50
Average	20.0	10.25	6.25	24.30	16.6	6.7

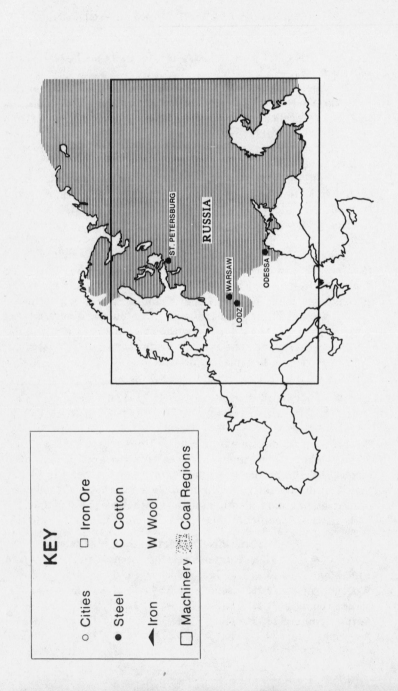

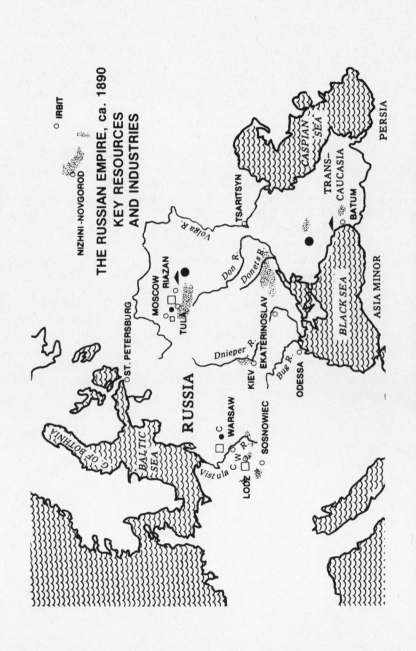

THE RUSSIAN EMPIRE, ca. 1890
KEY RESOURCES
AND INDUSTRIES

RUSSIA

○ IRBIT

NIZHNI-NOVGOROD ○

○ ST. PETERSBURG

BALTIC
SEA

G. OF BOTHNIA

MOSCOW
RIAZAN ●
TULA ○

Volga R.

Don R.

Donets R.

TSARITSYN

CASPIAN
SEA

TRANS-
CAUCASIA ○
BATUM

PERSIA

ASIA MINOR

BLACK SEA

Dnieper R.

KIEV ○

Bug R.

ODESSA ○

EKATERINOSLAV

WARSAW ● C
Vistula C W R.
LODZ
SOSNOWIEC ○

The difference for the textile industry in Lodz in comparison with Sosnowiec amounts to *+ 21.5 per cent for men, for women + 61.9 per cent, for children + 4.7 per cent.*

The real reason for the rise of industry in the Sosnowiec district, however, was the new era in Russian customs policy. Right after 1877, a whole series of Prussian and Saxon factories were simply moved from Germany to Poland. Considerable industry was soon concentrated in one zone of three Russian miles along the border. Of the 27 most significant factories which could be counted here in the vicinity of the border in 1886, five had been founded before 1877, 22 in 1877-1886 (81.5 per cent). The production of the factories in Sosnowiec amounted to one half million rubles in 1879, 13 million rubles in 1886, making an increase of 2,500 per cent in seven years.

The development of factory production in the Sosnowiec district went hand in hand with a surprising growth of the *coal industry*. Supported and, in the 1830s (1833-1842), even directly run by the Polish Bank, this industry developed quite slowly up until the 1860s and in 1860 produced a yield of 3.6 million poods of coal. Since this time, three important factors have come into play one after the other, which powerfully furthered the development of mining: first, the construction of railroads in the 1860s and 1870s, second, the development of factory industry, and third, the prohibitive tariff system. The upswing is expressed in the following figures:

Coal production, in millions of poods, was:

1860	3.6
1870	13.8
1880	78.4
1890	150.8

Thus, during the 20 years from 1870 to 1890, production had increased by 993 per cent.

The railroads form one of the most important buyers of coal. The Polish as well as the South Russian coal basin supply Russia's railways with fuel. The consumption of the latter amounted to:

THE INDUSTRIAL DEVELOPMENT OF POLAND

	In millions of poods		
	1880	**1885**	**1890**
of South Russian coal	22.2	34.3	39.8
of Polish coal	10.8	13.8	17.5

But factory industry is a still more important buyer of coal. In 1890 the Lodz district alone used 30.6 million poods of coal, the Warsaw district 26 million, and the Sosnowiec district 40 million poods, in which the iron works played a great role. In 1893, coal consumption in Warsaw came to 35.5 million poods, in Lodz in the same year 36.2 million, and in the year 1896 41 million poods.

A new epoch in the Polish coal industry begins with the extension of the protective tariff policy to this branch of production in 1884, which hit the until then duty-free import of foreign coal with a tariff of one half to two kopeks in gold per pood. The immediate result was a great "coal crisis" in Russia, i.e., a great coal shortage as a result of the backward methods of the Russian coal works and their inability to take the place of English coal with their own, relative to growing demand.

This was turned to the advantage of the Polish coal works, which rapidly expanded their activity and in a few years conquered all the important markets in Russia: Odessa, Moscow, St. Petersburg, even South Russia. Although the crisis has long since been overcome, Polish coal has since then beaten South Russian coal step-by-step out of the field in Russia, on the Moscow-Kursk, Moscow-Brest, Kiev-Voronesh, Fastow, St. Petersburg-Warsaw railway lines and in part on the southwestern lines. In 1894, 5,824,000 poods of coal came to Odessa from Poland, as against 5,300,000 from the South Russian basin.

It still remains to cast a glance at the district's iron industry. This has a longer history behind it, for already in the Duchy of Warsaw in the year 1814 there were 46 blast furnaces for iron ore. Development proceeded so slowly, however, that up to the 1880s Poland had not brought this industry beyond a production of 2.5 million poods of raw iron, 1.4 million poods of iron, and 3.9 million poods of steel.

A new page in the history of the Polish iron industry begins with the turn in Russian customs policy. The brief free-trade period after the Crimean War lasted somewhat longer for iron than for other commodities, since the Russian iron works could not have satisfied the enormous demand created by railway construction even with the strongest protective tariff policy. But since 1881, the protective tariff has taken the place of free trade here too, and after a gradual increase the customs rate was set in 1887 at 25 and 30 kopeks in gold per pood of raw iron, at 50 kopeks to 1.10 rubles for iron, and at 70 kopeks for steel; the tariff of 1891 brought a new increase in customs. As the immediate effect of the revision of the tariff we see the import of foreign metals to Russia decline in the following way:

	In millions of poods		
	Raw Iron	Iron	Steel
1881	14.3	6.5	1.4
1891	7.1	5.0	1.0

Correspondingly, metal production in Russia and Poland grew—in the latter, as follows:

	In millions of poods	
	Raw Iron	Iron and Steel
1860	0.7	0.3
1870	1.3(100%)	0.6(100%)
1880	2.4	5.5
1890	7.4(+488%)	7.5(+1054%)

The *third industrial district, the Warsaw district,* does not have so strongly stamped a physiognomy as the two already described. Here we find a great diversity of industrial branches, but the most important are *machine production* and the *sugar industry.* The history of the first is completely told in the following simple comparison. While until 1860 only nine factories producing agricultural machines existed in Poland, in 1860-1885 42 new ones were established. Here, as in all earlier cases, we see the same upswing as a result of the transformation of the market in the 1860s and 1870s.

Finally, let's take a look at the history of the sugar industry. It had already made its start in the 1820s, but until the 1850s was only a subsidiary branch of agriculture, of small dimensions and often run by the landowners themselves. The production of the 31 plants in operation in 1848 did not exceed 177,500 poods, amounting to no more than 5,000 to 6,000 poods per factory. The year 1854 shows the greatest number of sugar factories, when there were 55. Since the abolition of serfdom and the revolution in agriculture, sugar production severed itself from agriculture and became an independent branch of industry. The number of establishments gradually decreased through the simultaneous concentration of production. In 1870 we find still only 41 sugar factories with 1.2 million poods' annual production.

But a true revolution was brought about in the sugar industry by the tax and customs policy of the Russian government. Namely, in 1867 the singular system of sugar taxation which had applied in Poland until then was annulled and replaced by that of the Russian Empire. The latter was based on taxation not of the finished product actually produced, but on the amount of finished product which was assumed to be produced in every factory, measured by the fixed standard productivity of the press apparatus.

In this form the sugar tax naturally became the spur to the improvement of production; it soon moved all sugar factories to introduce the diffusion method, which pushed productivity above the norm taken as the basis for the tax, making the nominal tax of 80 kopeks per pood in reality only 35 or even 20. In 1876, to encourage sugar exports, the rebate on the excise on exported sugar was ordered, which in view of the above circumstances came to the same thing as a colossal export subsidy. This was yet another spur to a feverish improvement of production methods and to expansion of production.

In a few years the sugar industry in Russia and in Poland transformed themselves into large-scale industry. While Russia had only exported 4 poods of sugar in 1874, sugar exports in 1877 already amounted to 3,896,902 poods, for which the government had to "refund" roughly 3 million rubles — half of the entire sugar excise levied in the Empire. In 1881, the government took steps toward thorough reform of taxation of the sugar industry, but in the meantime the industry had reached very high levels of technological development. In Poland there were:

In 1869-70   41 factories with 1.2 million poods' production;
In 1890-91   40 factories with 4.8 million poods' production.

From this feverish expansion of production there followed a crisis in 1885, which brought in its wake the establishment of a sugar cartel embracing all of Russia and Poland, and so imprinted this branch of production with the clearest stamp of a large-scale industry. One fruit of this cartel is the fact that Russian sugar, whose production cost amounts to one and five-sixths *d* per pound, is bought outside the Empire for one and two-thirds *d*, but in Kiev for four *d* per pound. No wonder that with such monopoly prices the sugar factories are able to yield enormous dividends.

The foregoing picture of industry in Poland would not be complete if it were not at least supplemented with some information about the role of this industry in the economy of the Russian Empire in general and, in particular, in comparison with other important industrial districts. The significance of Poland and the two capitals of Russian factory production — St. Petersburg and Moscow — in terms of industrial activity can be generally represented by the following:

1890	Total Production (in millions of rubles)	Per Capita (in rubles)
Russian Empire	1,597	13.5
Moscow district	460	38
Petersburg district	242	40
Poland	210	23

As can be seen, Polish industry takes *third place* in the Empire, in absolute as well as in relative terms, while Moscow in absolute terms and Petersburg in relative terms claims first place. If we single out the two most important branches of production, textiles and mining, we obtain the following comparison:

Of the total production of the Empire (without Finland), which amounted to 82.0 million poods of raw iron, 25.7 million of iron, 34.5 million of steel, and 550 million of coal, the share falling to:

	Raw Iron	Iron	Steel	Coal
Ural district	36%	56%	7.7%	2.9%
Donets district	40%	6%	42.0%	54.0%
Poland	14%	14%	23.0%	40.0%

Specifically, in metal and coal production the Donets (South Russian) basin and the Urals are the most important Russian districts, and Poland is in competition with primarily the former but in part also with the latter for the Russian market. As we see, Poland stands in *second place* in the Empire in mining, right behind the Donets district, excluding the production of raw iron where it takes third place. Although Poland has only 7.3 per cent of the Empire's total population, it has a quarter of the Russian Empire's steel production and two-fifths of its coal production.

Similarly, in the Empire's textile industry, Poland plays a very significant role quite out of proportion with the size of its population. The share of the total number of spindles and looms in the Empire's cotton industry, which in 1886 amounted to 3,913,000 and 84,500 respectively, fell to:

	Spindles	Looms
Moscow district	55%	71.6%
Petersburg district	29%	12.8%
Poland	13%	12.5%

Here too Poland stands in *third* place. In the other brances it has a much greater significance, as is seen from the following: Of the total textile industry in the Empire, whose value of production amounted to 580.9 million rubles in 1892, 19.5 per cent fell to Poland; its share in individual branches, however, amounted in cotton spinning to 15.6 per cent, in cotton weaving to 16 per cent, in linen making to 42 per cent, in wool weaving and cloth making to 29.6 per cent, in wool spinning to 77 per cent, and in knitting to 78 per cent.

If Poland is on the whole outstripped by the industries of the central and Petersburg areas, nevertheless it leads all the other parts of the Empire in certain important branches of the economy. In particular, Poland's great significance in these branches points to a far-reaching division of labor between Polish and Russian industry.

1.5 Poland's Industrial Market

It has become clear from the foregoing that the Russian market forms the real mainspring of the current industrial development of Poland. It would therefore be interesting to hear more precise statements about the extent of the market for Polish commodities in Russia, but this can be determined only with difficulty. As in the statistics of all nations, there exists in those of Russia a great lack of data on internal trade. Here an overview can be obtained only indirectly and approximately. The official inquiry which took place in 1886 showed that of the 141 largest factories, which together represent a third of all production,

37 factories with 7,061,984 rubles produce exclusively for Poland,

27 factories with 7,480,645 rubles produce exclusively for Russia,

11 factories with 13,224,589 rubles produce chiefly for Poland,

34 factories with 22,824,013 rubles produce chiefly for
    Russia,
32 factories with 19,311,695 rubles produce half for Poland
    and half for Russia.

If we assume the expression "chiefly" to be equivalent to two-thirds, then Polish industry's market can be represented as follows: The 141 factories produce commodities

for Poland to the value of 33,142,228 rubles, equaling 47%;
for Russia to the value of 36,760,698 rubles, equaling 52%.

The general conclusion reached by the commission of inquiry was that Polish factories sell 50 to 55 per cent of their products in Russia.

This conclusion also confirms particular statements on the market for the city of Lodz's textile industry. These were:

	In poods					
	1884 (crisis)		1885		1886	
	Poland	Russia	Poland	Russia	Poland	Russia
Cotton and wool cloth	372,390	1,004,286	321,344	1,115,460	443,565	1,507,259
Yarn	45,290	4,524	63,051	99,951	56,583	90,136
Total	417,680	1,008,810	384,395	1,215,411	500,148	1,597,395

Thus the center of the textile industry was already selling three-fourths of its products in Russia by the middle of the 1880s. In the ten years since the above calculations were made, however, it is probable that this situation has shifted in much greater measure in favor of sales in Russia, since production has grown by roughly half again since then, while the domestic market has obviously been able to increase only relatively little. On the other hand we have direct evidence that the Polish market opened up new areas in Russia during these ten years, about which we will have more to say later. Thus one can assume as the minimum situation today that two-thirds of the products of Polish industry are absorbed by Russia. Specifically, this market encompasses those branches of industry which form the main stem of large-scale capitalist production in any country: the textile, metal, and coal industries. Naturally a whole series of smaller industrial branches, such as sugar and fancy-goods production, tanning, etc., are also sending their products to Russia in ever growing amounts.

The advance of the Polish market in Russia offers an interesting picture from a geographical standpoint. As was said, this trade began in larger scale only in the 1870s. For a long time, however, it was restricted to only the western and southern gubernias of the Empire — to Lithuania and the Ukraine, thus actually to the old parts of what was then Poland. But in the beginning of the 1880s, Poland conquered a new market in Russia's south, in so-called New Russia. In the middle of the 1880s, Polish trade makes another step forward. In 1883 the free transit to the Transcaucasus via Batum, agreed to in the Berlin Congress, was abolished and a tariff border erected. With this the Western European countries, above all England, lost a significant market for their products, a market which now went over to Russian and Polish industrialists. In the year 1885, Polish manufactured goods appeared for the first time in the Caucasus; since that time their import of these goods to the three centers of Caucasian trade has grown as follows:

	In poods		
	Batum	Tiflis	Baku
1885-86	39,000	55,000	68,000
1887-88	95,100	200,000	258,000

At the end of the 1880s Polish trade pushed to the northeast—to the Volga region. Polish imports to the center of Volga trade, *Tsaritsyn,* were:

1887	55,640 poods;
1888	73,729 poods;
1889	106,403 poods.

At the same time Poland began to take part in European-Asiatic trade; its products appeared in the two colossal annual fairs in *Nizhni-Novgorod*, where large Polish warehouses were built beginning in 1889, and in *Irbit*. Finally, in the end of the 1880s and the beginning of the 1890s, Polish trade steps onto Asian ground. First, trade relations were entered into with Siberia: in 1888 with *Tomsk* in West Siberia, in 1892 with Nerchinsk in southeastern Siberia, in 1894 Polish commodities appear in

Omsk. During the same time, Polish trade in Asia also deve ps in two other directions, on the one hand to China, on the other to Persia and Asia Minor.

In the course of 20 years, 1870-1890, Polish trade found access step-by-step to every corner of European Russia. This rapid expansion of the market, as we have seen, turned Polish factory production into large-scale industry in 20 years. Since then, however, it has been preparing itself for a new, important undertaking — *the conquest of Asian markets*. Polish trade has already made several important steps in this direction. This, however, is doubtless only the beginning of a beginning, and the tremendous prospects that are opening to industry thanks to the Trans-Siberian Railway and the powerful effect of Russian policy in Asia mean for Polish industry (among other things) a new revolution, a revolution perhaps even more thoroughgoing than that which it experienced in the 1870s. Polish entrepreneurs are preparing themselves in all seriousness for this future, and turn their attention persistently to Asia. A museum of the East has been built in Warsaw, which has the special task of making manufacturers thoroughly familiar with the commodities, the tastes, and the requirements of Asia. The prospectus of the new institution reports:

"Sugar and brandy, machines and pipe, glass, faience, and porcelain, shoes, cravats, and gloves, shawls, cotton and linen, which are made here did not go further than to a neighboring gubernia not long ago; today they travel over the Don, the Urals, to the Caucasus, over the Caspian Sea, to China, Persia, and Asia Minor. But in order to extend this as far as possible, our taste cannot be imposed on those for whom the goods are intended; rather they must be adapted to, we must produce what will sell in those markets, where, however, taste is endlessly different from our own...The type of cloth, the form, the pattern, the favorite colors are different there than here...That which we have produced until now was preeminently intended for the civilized emigrant population layers of those countries. The *masses* stand outside the scope of our industry. However, if we want to produce goods which correspond to the taste and the customs of the masses, and therefore we must become acquainted with the needs of these masses."

This in brief outline is the history of industry in Russian

THE INDUSTRIAL DEVELOPMENT OF POLAND

Poland. Beginning with the efforts of the Kingdom of Poland, it attempts from the first moment to take possession of the Russian market. Then, with access to those markets impeded, industry develops slowly and step-by-step. The social crisis which Russia experienced in the 1860s also tears Poland out of its economic stasis and drags it into the whirlpool of capitalist development. With the renewed and this time permanent opening up of the Russian market, Polish industry gains very fertile ground and quickly goes through the process of transformation into large-scale industry. Russia's tariff policy monopolizes the favors of this enormous market area for Russian and Polish capitalists and engenders feverish capital accumulation. Factory industry becomes the leading factor of Poland's entire social life, in which a total revolution also occurs in the last 25 years.

As we have mentioned above, until the 1860s Poland preserved the character of an agricultural country dominated by the landowner class in all areas of public life. The Peasant Reform diminished to a great extent this predominance of noble landed property. The necessity of laying out the money capital now indispensable for operations heavily increased its indebtedness. The supervening general crisis in European agriculture in the 1880s and the fall in the price of grain finished it off.

The whole broad layer of medium-sized noble landed property thus moved, and moves, closer to its own ruin every day. Fifteen per cent of aristocratic property has already passed out of the hands of its owners and into German and Jewish hands; another 15 per cent has been broken up into parcels and sold to peasants. The remaining landed property is burdened with mortgages amounting to 80 per cent of the value on the average, but in two-fifths of the cases to 100 up to 250 per cent. But at the same time, industry grew stronger and stronger, and soon it was to overtake agriculture in all respects. Already in 1880 the value of industrial production was equal to that of grain production. Today it has surpassed grain production by more than double; the former amounts to at least 23 rubles per capita, the latter only 11 rubles. Furthermore, this quantitatively inferior agriculture is wholly reduced to dependence on industry. While Poland was then "a European granary," a country producing grain principally for the world market, it now hardly satisfies its own needs. Industry created an internal market which devours the entire farm product. If today Poland still exports considerable quantities of wheat, this happens only because she imports still greater quantities of lesser kinds of grain from Russia as substitute. Secondly, in view of the constantly falling price of grain, agriculture today sees itself forced to emancipate itself altogether from pure wheat production and to devote itself more and more to the cultivation of so-called technical crops for industry as well as cattle-breeding. It is unnecessary to emphasize that handicraft too, where it has not been destroyed directly by the competition of factories, on the contrary lives on factory industry — in part working for it directly, in part profiting from the accumulation of capital and growth in the domestic market which industry brought about. Industry has now become the stem from which all other branches of the country's material existence draw their life's blood. Or better put, it is the mainspring around which all aspects of material existence revolve and subordinate themselves: agriculture, handicraft, trade, and transportation. Poland, once the country so very unique in its social relations, has become a typical capitalist country. The mechanical loom and the steam engine have robbed her of her original physiognomy and imprinted on her a leveling international character. Already in 1884, Poland suffered the specifically capitalist disease — its first big crisis. Today, here and there in the awakening labor movement, Polish capitalism's Hypocratic characteristics are emerging as well.

Part 2

Russia's Economic Policy in Poland

The picture given thus far of the development and present state of industry in Poland is completely different from that offered by the history of the urban trades in the Poland of the Middle Ages. Despite the identical nature of their origins — artificial, governmental transplanting from Germany — manufacture in Poland not only did not perish, as had urban handicraft earlier, but developed itself into heavy industry. And despite its foreign German beginnings, it not only drove deep roots into Poland's national life, but actually became the ruling, tone-setting factor.

Only recently certain phenomena have appeared which have awakened fears on many sides about the continued future of Polish industry. It is clear that the market in Russia, and in connection with that the market opened up since then in Asia, forms the mainspring of Polish industry. In all these areas, however, Polish products are of course in competition with

123

Russian goods. A natural conflict of interest between the Russian and Polish bourgeoisies over these markets appears at first glance to result, a conflict that must become harsher the more Polish industry grows. On the other hand, it seems to be just as natural for the Russian capitalist class to have the Russian government on its side against the Polish competition, that the government could use its power to the disadvantage of Polish industry, and perhaps erect a tariff barrier between Poland and Russia once more as the simplest and most ruthless means of effecting this. Such ideas have made themselves very much heard recently, and here and there the opinion is expressed that after the prevailing period of prosperity a period of persecution and punishment from the side of the Russian government has begun for Polish industry, which will sooner or later go under.

Therefore, before we conclude the description of Polish industry, we must go into the question of what significance the conflict of interest between Polish and Russian factory production in fact has, what the preparations of Polish industry are in its competitive battle with Russian industry, and what the position of the Russian government toward this struggle is. In this way, we will be in a position to complete the history of industry in Poland through a perspective on its future.

2.1 The History of the Struggle Between Lodz and Moscow

Above all, it is totally untrue that the competition and the struggle between the central and the Polish industrial districts, the struggle about which so much fuss was made a few years ago, is a new phenomenon dating only from the 1880s, as is generally assumed. Quite the contrary: this battle is as old as Polish industry itself. Already in the 1820s, the government was presented with petitions which from the Russian side concerned the increase of the Russian-Polish tariffs, from the Polish side the total abolition of the tariff barrier between Poland and Russia. Since then, the rivalry has never really ceased. Excluding the year 1826, there were 1,831 petitions from Russian entrepreneurs sent to St. Petersburg — always with complaints about Polish industry and with demands for support for the "Fatherland's" industry in its fight against the Polish. As one observes from the history of Polish industry, in the end, the government not only did not fulfill the requests of the Russian entrepreneurs, but, on the contrary, abolished the tariff border between Poland and Russia in 1851 and so let the contest between the enemy industries take its own course. The battle flared up intensely and anew in the middle of the 1880s, first because Polish industry at this time — as was mentioned — took possession of a whole series of new market areas in Russia, in the south as well as the east, and second, because, just at that time, the whole textile industry of the Sosnowiec district was seemingly conjured up out of the ground at the Prussian border. But, on the other hand, the price of goods, forced up suddenly and severely by the change in tariff policies at the end of the 1870s, had fallen somewhat toward the middle of the 1880s. The Moscow entrepreneurs, upset by this, began "to seek out the guilty party," and found it, too — Polish competition. Here the battle was led chiefly by the Moscow cotton manufacturers, in the face of the conquest of Russian markets by Polish cotton goods.

A certain *Sharapov* led the first attack from the side of the Moscow entrepreneurs in a public speech which he gave in Moscow and in Ivanovo-Voznesenski in 1885 and which later appeared in print. From the start, Sharapov struck the keynotes and puffed up the whole campaign of Moscow cotton versus Lodz fustian into an historic duel between the Slavic and German races. He demonstrated that Polish industry in every way enjoyed more favorable conditions than Russian industry; for example, according to Sharapov, cheaper German credit was at Poland's disposal — it paid 3.5 to 4 per cent, while the entrepreneurs in central Russia had to pay 7 to 8 per cent. Second, cheaper raw materials were available to Poland, which also had to bear far lower transportation costs than the Moscow districts lying far to the east; third, Poland enjoyed more favorable railway rates, which it obtained as a result of the private agreement among the railway companies; fourth and finally, it had significantly lower taxes to pay: in the central district amounting to 3,600 rubles per 1 million rubles of production, in Lodz however 1,400 rubles, and in small Polish cities only 109 rubles.

Sharapov called the government to battle against the "German" industry of Poland and to the rescue of the Russian and *Polish* elements oppressed by it (!).

The next year, 1886, the Moscow entrepreneurs ordered a deputation to St. Petersburg with the "most humble and obedient" request to once again establish a tariff line between Poland and Russia.

The government, thus approached, formed a commission in the same year, 1886, consisting of Professors Yanshul, Ilyin, and Langowoi, which had the task of investigating the conditions of production of the Polish industrial districts and of checking into the claims of Moscow manufacturers and their correctness. The results of this investigation, carried out more seriously and more thoroughly than any other, was the following.

On the side of Polish industry we see cheaper fuel, smaller fixed capital, lower taxes, a better labor force, and more advantageous spatial concentrations of firms in a few spots. On the side of Russian industry, on the other hand, cheaper labor power, smaller transportation costs to the markets (Caucasus, Volga region, Asia), smaller outlays on the workforce (hospitals, schools, etc.), profits from the factory stores, finally a surplus of water to run the cotton weaving and spinning mills. In conclusion, the commission came out against the introduction of a tariff line between Poland and Russia, and likewise against a differential tariff on raw cotton directed against Poland, first because the government "would hardly deem it possible to treat Poland as a foreign country in trade and industrial relations," and second because a higher differential tariff "would appear to the inhabitants of Poland, Russian subjects, as an injustice against them and would doubtless give rise to great dissatisfaction." The commission considered the only just measure to be an increase in the prevailing taxes on Polish industry sufficient to equalize them with Russian taxes.

In 1887, the Moscow entrepreneurs once more presented a petition to the Finance Minister at the annual fair in Nizhni-Novgorod, in which they requested the increase in the duties on cotton and the introduction of a higher differential tariff at the Polish border. Now the Lodz manufacturers also entered the fray. They answered the above-mentioned document with a counter-petition, in which they sought to prove that they suffered significantly less advantageous conditions of production than their Moscow competitors, that the cotton mills of the central district yielded up to 8.4 per cent profits while those in Poland yielded only 7.5 per cent, that transport of raw cotton from Liverpool to Moscow cost 35.77 kopeks per pood but from

Liverpool to Lodz 37.10 kopeks per pood, that therefore a further worsening of their situation by the introduction of a differential tariff on cotton would make cotton production extremely difficult for them.

In 1888, a commission was once again set up under the chairmanship of Ber to investigate the dispute. Its conclusions this time were very much to Poland's disadvantage, and the commission called for a series of measures to protect the Moscow industrial district against better situated Polish industry. Meanwhile, the Moscow industrialists again submitted a petition to the Finance Minister in 1888, in which they complained about their pressing situation and demanded measures from the government against "parasitical" Polish industry.

The Lodz industrialists published an agitational piece in 1889 under the title, "Moscow's Battle with Lodz," in which they attempted to show through the mouth of "an impartial, nonpartisan observer" that Lodz had to pay more for raw cotton than did Moscow, that the advantage of cheaper fuel which Lodz had over Moscow only came to the negligible amount of 0.2 kopeks per arshin of material, that the origins of Moscow's more expensive credit lay with Moscow itself, and that it was because of insufficient organization that Lodz suffered from a shortage of water, paid more for labor, and finally, made smaller profits than central Russian industry.

In 1890, the organization and nationalization of the railway tariff system undertaken by the government gave rise once more to the convocation of a new commission. This commission was to investigate, for the xth time, what the state of the competitive conditions of the Polish and central Russian industrial districts was, and how, relative to this, the railway fares for the lines of importance to the competitors should be figured. This commission, which functioned under the chairmanship of the representative of the railway department, Lazarev, again came to no conclusion. The representatives of the Lodz and Moscow industrialists gave their well-known arguments and counterarguments as best they could. Two arguments from the Polish side were the only new additions, namely, their reference to the use of cheap naphtha residue as fuel in the Moscow industrial district, and the claim that the tax burden was greater in Poland than in central Russia, specifically 5.82 rubles per member of the population in the latter, but in the former 6.64 rubles.

However the next year, 1891, a well-known economist, Belov, was authorized to investigate the conditions of production in Poland and central Russia. This too came to the conclusion that all the disadvantages were on the Lodz side, while all the advantages were on Moscow's: specifically, cheaper labor power, longer labor time (Moscow 3,429 hours a year, Poland 3,212), cheaper fuel (naphtha residue costs 6 d per cwt, whereas coal for the same amount of heat is significantly more, 10.25 per cwt), cheaper raw cotton, and finally, more favorable railway fares. The same Shaparov who had sounded the first alarm against Lodz in 1885 now claimed as a result of the Belov investigation that the situation had completely changed since 1885 and that Lodz now absolutely did not deserve to be punished in any way.

It was necessary to treat the various stages of the dispute between Lodz and Moscow so thoroughly in order to show how difficult it is to form an unbiased opinion on this question, and how carefully claims about this point usually must be taken. For there is not a single argument which was not brought up by both parties, with directly contradictory figures as proof, and it is only too easy to unconsciously become a mouthpiece for one of these two industrialists' choirs.

Now that we have become acquainted in brief with the story of the Moscow-Lodz dispute and the main points around which it centers, we ourselves will compare the competitive conditions of the two industries with each other in all the main points, in order to achieve an objective grasp of the problem on the basis of quantitative evidence.

2.2 Conditions of Industrial Production in Poland and in Russia

1. Fuel. One of the, by far, most important conditions of production for any factory industry is fuel. For Polish industry, this factor is seen by many researchers as the decisive one in its development, and is regarded as the most important in its competitive struggle with Russian industry. So says the report of the above-mentioned commission of 1886: "Fuel is doubtless that factor of production which makes up the most important difference in the conditions of production of the central gubernias and the Kingdom of Poland."

Polish industry possesses large and rich collieries, while the center of Russian industry, the Moscow district, lies far away from the collieries of the Donets area and is in the main forced to rely on more expensive wood or peat. "The price of wood in the Moscow gubernia is higher every day, and according to the calculation of Engineer Belikov, costs on the average 11.6 to 13.1 kopeks per pood of wood. Peat, whose use in the factories is growing rapidly and which is already being used in Moscow to the extent of 100,000 cords annually, comes to 12 and even 16 kopeks per pood, mainly due to high transport costs, and its use is in any case only to a factory's advantage if it is in the close vicinity of the peatbog."

In Moscow, Russian coal costs 13.3 kopeks (from Tula), 17.5 (from Riazan), and 25 (from the Donets area). English coal also costs 25 kopeks per pood. "How much more relatively expensive the most-used fuels, wood and peat, are — given at the same time the impossibility of replacing them by still more expensive coal — and how vital this question is for Russian industry, can be judged by the following: Average heat production, according to the account of the same Engineer Belikov, is 2,430 degrees (F.C.) to 2,700 degrees for wood, for Moscow peat 1,920 to 2,800 degrees; the same heat production for coal is 3,280 degrees for that from Tula, but for coal from Donets and for English coal it goes far above 5,000 degrees."

In this connection, Polish industry finds itself in a quite different situation. The average price of coal in the main centers of industry — Sosnowiec, Lodz, and Warsaw — are: 2.4-4.95 kopeks, 11.5 kopeks, and 13 kopeks per pood, thus less than wood in Moscow, while heat production is of course significantly greater.

Calculated per unit of product, outlays for fuel amount to:

per pood of cotton yarn		
in Poland	in Moscow	in St. Petersburg
38 kopeks	90 kopeks	53 kopeks

These figures suffice to show the great advantage that Polish industry has in regard to fuel over its Russian competition.

Professor Schulze-Gävernitz nevertheless believes it possible to say that "natural advantages are of no benefit to Polish industry. Certainly cheaper fuel is pointed to, but according to Mendeleyev's data, compared with the above-mentioned report, this advantage declines to the extent that Moscow goes over to naphtha fuel (one pood of bituminous coal in Lodz 12-13 kopeks, the same heat value in naphtha 12.75 kopeks)."

On that, the following should be noted. First, a pood of bituminous coal does not cost 12-13 kopeks in Lodz, as Professor Schulze-Gävernitz says, but 8.75-13.5 (or, 8.3-14.7), and a pood of naphtha coal, i.e., a quantity of naphtha corresponding calorifically to a pood of coal, costs not 12.75 kopeks, but 13-20 kopeks, thus significantly more than coal in Poland. Second, for the present, naphtha makes up only 20.5 per cent of all fuel in the Moscow district — in particular, 29.4 per cent in the cotton industry in the Moscow and,Vladimir gubernias — and so cannot influence the conditions of production among the overwhelming majority of the factories in these districts.

But third, as far as the future of this fuel method, Professor Mendeleyev says in his essay dedicated to the naphtha industry: "The use of this (naphtha residue) as a fuel today, where there is no possibility of utilizing the bulk of the naphtha obtained (as a result of the lack of a pipeline to carry naphtha from Baku to Batum), is the most natural phenomenoñ, although a unique and temporary one." "For normal fuel needs, particularly for fueling steam engines, where any sort of fuel is suitable, *the use of a fuel as costly as naphtha residue can find wide circulation only temporarily, in those transitional moments of industrial activity in the nation where industry has not had the time to arrange a proper bed for itself;* but today in all countries that presumes as its condition — the use of coal."

And still further. "The use today of 130 million poods of naphtha residue in Russia *must be regarded as a temporary phenomenon*, which depends, on the one side, on the lack of a market for naphtha on the world market, and, on the other, on the lack of productivity in the extraction of coal and of its distribution throughout Russia, particularly in the center and the southeast." "The construction of railway lines from the Donets coal district to the Volga, and various measures directed toward utilization of naphtha supplies in Baku and toward cheap export of coal from Donets, form the current tasks of Russia's industrial development, and *must make an end to today's irrational, widespread use of naphtha residue from Baku for steam boilers."*

The above quotations, which express the opinion of the best judges on this question, suffice in our opinion to demonstrate that in the comparative valuation of fuels in Poland and in Moscow, naphtha fuel in the latter must be disregarded, as a temporary phenomenon. What is now called "naphtha residue" is not some actual production by-product, but the product of the naphtha extraction itself, which is very insufficiently utilized only as a result of the lack of a market, and to a great extent used for fuel rather than lighting: thus among exports from Baku, for every pood of naphtha in, for example, the year 1891 there corresponds 1.40 poods of naphtha residue, and in 1894 as much as 2.73 poods. Thus, the so-called residue actually forms the main product, naphtha on the other hand the by-product.

The abnormality of this phenomenon appears in the quality of the product itself. The "residue" so obtained explodes at 50 degrees, 40 degrees, and even 30 degrees centigrade, while the normal explosion temperature for actual naphtha residue cannot be lower than 140-120 degrees. Thus, also, the costly results of cheap fuel: in the course of the years 1893 and 1894, 20 vessels of the Astrakhan Steamship Company that were fueled with "residue" were destroyed by outbreaks of fire. Another disadvantage of naphtha fuel is the fact that this residue, because of its chemical composition, is in fact used in much greater quantities to produce a specific effective heat than should be the case with real naphtha residue. The larger consumption of "residue" sometimes amounts to 40 per cent, and was confirmed by the administration of the Petersburg-Moscow railway line as an established phenomenon.

This makes the most important advantage of naphtha fuel — its cheapness — for the most part completely illusory. Here and there some are already beginning to renounce the use of naphtha residue, as with the Russian South-East railway, which recently returned to coal. Certainly the consumption of naphtha residue in the central industrial district will in the next few years increase before it will decrease, particularly as a result of overproduction and lower prices. With the Russian government's current vigor in promoting capitalism and pushing aside all obstacles in its way, however, the use of naphtha will soon be reduced to its rational purpose, and factories will be reduced to using wood and coal. In the end, however, Poland's advantage remains in full force, for "in general fuel is half as expensive in Poland as in Moscow."

2. Labor Power. This aspect of industrial activity is usually cited as proof that Poland has less favorable conditions than does Russia because its labor is more expensive than the latter's. Wages are in fact significantly higher in Poland than in Russia, specifically:

	Cotton Spinning	Cotton Weaving	Finishing	Wool-Spinning
for men	18.75%	36%	19%	59%
for women	42%	37%	107%	91%
for children	14%	79%	85%	27%

	Wool Weaving	Cloth-Making	Half-wool Weaving	Average
for men	31%	13%	60%	32.2%
for women	105%	33%	122%	73.9%
for children	112%	40%	150%	60.0%

Labor time, on the other hand, is significantly longer in Russia than in Poland. "While 13- to 14-hour-long labor is very widespread in Moscow factories, in Poland it is to be found only in nine factories, and in three of these cases only in separate factory sections. While labor time lasting more than 14 hours is absolutely not a rarity in Moscow factories and its outer limit is 16 hours, 14-hour labor time must be described as the outer limit in Poland, and in fact this was found only in two cloth factories." In general ten to 12 hours were worked in 75 per cent of the factories; thus 11 hours can be taken as the average labor time for Poland. In Moscow, the average labor time is more than 12 hours. In Poland, night labor is a rare exception; in Moscow it is widespread. And despite the fact that in Poland the number of workdays in the year is 292, while in Moscow it amounts to 286, for Poland there are nevertheless only 3,212 labor-hours per year, while the number in Moscow (figured on the basis of only 12 hours a day) is 3,430 hours, thus 218 hours more.

These two factors, lower wages and long labor time, are usually regarded as important advantages for Moscow industry in its competitive struggle with Polish manufacturing. Yet we believe that this opinion can be shown to be premature and superficial.

First, in comparing wages, usually the wages of male workers in Russia are juxtaposed to those of male workers in Poland, while likewise the wages of female workers in Russia are compared to those of female workers in Poland. This is how the 1886 commission for the investigation of Polish industry, among others, proceeded. This is wrong, as factory inspector Sviatlovski perceived, insofar as, in Poland, female and child labor is far more extensive than in Russia, so that frequently a female worker in Poland stands counterposed to a male worker in Russia; therefore, the wages of male Russian workers must frequently be compared with not those of *male* but of female Polish workers. In fact, the number of women employed in the Polish textile industry (the industry of most importance to the question of competition) amounts to more than 50 per cent of all factory personnel, while, in the Moscow district, female labor amounts to only 37 per cent in the cotton industry and only 28 per cent in the wool industry.

If the wages of male workers in Russia are compared with those of female workers in Poland, the picture shifts in many ways to the disadvantage of the Moscow district, or in any case there is an equalization of conditions. The average monthly wages in the textile industry are (in rubles):

	in Poland	in Russia
for men	20.1	15.2
for women	15.3	8.8
for children	8.8	5.5

To obtain true and exact data on relative wage levels in Russia and Poland, it is necessary to consider the composition of the labor force in terms of age and sex in both countries as well as nominal wages. The result thus attained will be in many ways significantly different than the foregoing. This above all is the corrective that should be applied to the usual conclusions drawn from the comparison of wages.

Second, the fact that the Russian worker frequently receives lodging (and here and there even board) from the factory is often disregarded. This applies not only to single but also to married workers, whose families usually live in the same factory barracks. Here heating fuel is likewise provided by the factory. This should be figured into the wages of Russian workers if one wants to make an exact comparison. Thus, the difference even in nominal wages is not so greatly to Poland's disadvantage as would appear from a more superficial comparison.

But far more important are further factors which show that factory labor in Poland is significantly *more intensive* than in Russia.

THE INDUSTRIAL DEVELOPMENT OF POLAND

The Polish worker is first of all more intelligent and better educated, on the average. Insofar as Professor Yanshul investigated this question, it was shown that in the central district the number of workers who could read and write amounted to 22 to 36 per cent of the total, in Poland to 45 to 65 per cent.

Furthermore, the Polish worker is better fed than the Russian worker, and this is especially true for women. Third, the workforce in Poland is a stable layer of the population, devoted exclusively to factory labor. In Russia, an observable, although gradually decreasing, portion of the workforce is still made up of peasants who return to the land in the summer and exchange precise factory work for crude farm labor.

Fourth, the Polish worker is far more individualized in his way of life than the Russian. As was already mentioned, the latter in many cases lives in factory barracks and is allotted board by the factory. Such a way of life, under certain circumstances, leads to the stunting of individuality. The Russian worker thus remains constantly under the control of his master and is bound by the factory rules even in his private life. The Moscow factory inspector knew of factories where, he reported, singing — whether in workplace or living quarters — is punished by a fine of five rubles; likewise workers incur a high fine when they pay each other a visit, and so forth. Not infrequently, workers are assigned to an apartment in a damp factory cellar, or in rooms that are so mean that one almost has to go on all fours to get into them. In Poland, the situation is different: the worker always runs his own household, and his housing is significantly better overall.

According to the unanimous opinion of all researchers who have made wage labor the subject of their investigation, all the cited factors — education, better housing and food, individual households — in short, everything which raises the living standard of the worker, are of decisive significance for the intensity of his activity.

Finally, piece-rate wages predominate in Poland, which, it is recognized, raises the intensity of labor to the utmost, while in Russia the time wage predominates.

All the above-mentioned factors make it apparent that the labor of Polish factory workers is far more intensive in comparison to that of Russian workers. And this characteristic of the

Polish worker so greatly outweighs his higher nominal wages and shorter work time, that he *turns out to be cheaper to the Polish factory owner than the Russian worker is* to his employer.

Reckoned per pood, wages amount to:

	In rubles	
	for cotton fabrics	for cotton yarn
in Poland	0.77-1.50	0.66-1.20
in Russia	2 and more	0.80-1.50

The difference in the length of the workday in Poland and Russia belongs to the past now that the workday has recently been reduced by law to 11.5 hours. However, the new measure will primarily be to the advantage of the Polish industrialists in their competitive struggle, perhaps for years to come, even if it will, in time, doubtless become a spur to technical development for the Moscow district. For the Russian worker's productivity, whose lower level depends on so many other factors, will obviously not increase overnight. Just how justified this conclusion is is shown by the fact that already in 1892 the Polish factory owners — in part to show a friendly face to the workers, who in May of that year had mounted an impressive strike in Lodz — went to the government with the request that the workday be reduced to 11 hours throughout the Empire, a project which foundered primarily because of the resistance of the Moscow industrialists.

3. Composition of capital. This important factor is also differently shaped in Poland than in Moscow. In Poland, a firm's sum of fixed capital is in most cases exceeded by the value of its yearly production, sometimes even two or three times, but on the average the relationship of fixed capital to the value of production is 2:3.2. In Russia, particularly in the central district, this relationship is inverted. Here the value of production (in the same branches of production) is often smaller than fixed capital, at most the same, and only seldom significantly higher. This phenomenon stems from two circumstances. First, far more is spent on buildings for enterprises in Russia than in Poland, because construction materials are very significantly more expensive. Second, however, because the great majority of factories in Russia include their own factory barracks, which never occurs in Poland.

If, therefore, what Marx calls the "organic composition of capitals" (the relationship of the constant to the variable portion of capital) is "higher" in Russia than in Poland, this has absolutely nothing to do with the higher stage of development of Russian production, but on the contrary with its primitive plant, for the most part. This makes necessary a series of expenditures which have nothing to do with the actual production process. As a result — all other conditions of production and sale being equal — the Polish industrialists are able to realize a surplus profit from the sale of their goods on the Russian market, in comparison with the Russian entrepreneurs. In addition, Polish labor, as was shown, is far more intensive.

4. *The turnover period* of capital is much shorter in Poland than in Russia. First, reserves of fuel and raw materials are stocked for long periods. The high prices and the general shortage of fuel in inner Russia mean, for the Russian entrepreneur, the necessity of laying out large sums of money for the purchase of forests or peat bogs. In this way, almost every large Moscow factory has put more or less considerable dead capital into forests and bogs. In addition, wood and especially peat are cheaply and easily delivered only in winter; therefore every Moscow factory lays in reserves of these fuels for a full year, even for two years. In Poland, because of the short distances involved, stocks of coal are laid in for only one to four weeks, at most for three months. Similarly, in Russia stocks of raw materials, particularly cotton, are laid in for lengthy periods, in Poland only for two to six months.

Second, the Polish industrialist realizes his product much more quickly than does the Russian entrepreneur. The Poles grant their customers only three to six months' credit, the Russians 12 to 18 months. The Poles — following the English and German model — produce on orders obtained by their traveling agents; the Russians produce according to their own estimates, often stocking for two or three years. This factor also signifies that Polish industrial capital — all other things being equal — is better armed for competitive struggle.

5. *The concentration of production* is significantly greater in Poland than in Russia. The value of production per factory in those branches of industry not levied with excise duties averaged in rubles:

	1885	1886	1887	1888	1889	1890
in Russia	50,824	52,248	54,601	58,237	58,972	57,578
in Poland	57,875	63,860	71,894	74,051	71,305	71,248

The difference is still greater if particular branches of production are compared. In the coal industry, for example, the situation is as follows. If the number of pits and shafts as well as the quantity of production in Russia are taken to be 100, then one finds in Poland in 1890 6.8 per cent pits, 6.2 per cent shafts, 70.6 per cent production.

With a number of shafts 16 times smaller, therefore, coal extraction in Poland equals more than eleven-sixteenths of Russian coal extraction. Eighty-five per cent of the quantity of the entire yearly production of the Dabrova district (1893) is yielded by five firms.

In other branches, such as the cotton industry, the gross product per factory is greater in Russia. The smaller concentration of this sort of production in Poland has to do with special circumstances, however, which to go into here would lead us into too much detail and which in any case have nothing to do with the degree of technological development. On the contrary, in Poland, as we will soon see, the yearly value of production per worker is in this as in most branches greater than in Russia.

6. *The technology* of production, lastly, forms the most important difference between Polish and Russian industry. We will compare the most significant branches of production in both countries in terms of technology.

To begin with the textile branch: first the cotton industry shows:

1890	Factories	Spindles	Looms	Steam Horsepower
Russia	351	2,819,326	91,545	38, 750
Poland	94	472,809	11,084	13,714

1890	Production (in thousands of rubles)	Workers: Male	Female
Russia	208,581	103,916	83,941
Poland	31,495	10,474	9,535

The technical superiority of the Polish cotton industry is clear from the above comparison. In comparison with the

Russian industry, it has: *10 per cent of the workers, 15 per cent of the production, 35 per cent of the steam power.*

For every worker there is 1,110 rubles production yearly in Russia, 1,574 rubles in Poland, that is, 42 per cent more. Steam power amounts to 204 for every 1,000 workers in Russia, to 186 for every 1 million rubles of production; it amounts to 685 for every 1,000 workers in Poland, to 439 for every 1 million rubles of production, thus 236 per cent and 136 per cent more, respectively, in Poland.

Finally, the use of female labor is greater in Poland than in Russia. In the latter, female workers make up 44.7 per cent of the personnel, in the former 47.6 per cent. According to other accounts which we noted above, and which inspire more confidence because they were determined not by summary bureaucratic statistics but by a special commission, the use of female labor in Poland is much higher, and in Russia, on the contrary, much lower.

Roughly the same result is obtained by comparing the *wool industry* in Poland and in Russia. This shows:

1890	Factories	Spindles	Looms	Steam Horsepower
Russia	164	77,474	11,784	2,230
Poland	168	245,892	4,016	6,667

1890	Production (in thousands of rubles)	Workers: Male	Female
Russia	21,585	14,471	7,050
Poland	26,199	8,486	6,670

For Poland, in comparison with Russia, this comes out to: *Workers 70.4 per cent, production 121 per cent, steam power 299 per cent;* thus for every worker in Russia 1,003 rubles production annually, for every worker in Poland 1,729 rubles, that is, 72 per cent more. Steam power amounts to 104 for every 1,000 workers in Russia, to 103 for every 1 million rubles of production; it amounts to 440 for every 1,000 workers in Poland, to 254 for every 1 million rubles of production.

Thus, if we take 100 as the number for the steampower per 1,000 workers or 1 million rubles of production in Russia, then we find the same in Poland to be 323 per cent and 146 per cent more, respectively. In the use of female labor, we see here an even greater difference between Poland and Russia than in the cotton industry, specifically 32.7 per cent female workforce in Russia, 44 per cent in Poland. The technical superiority of the Polish textile industry is even more evident in the fact that higher grades of spinning yarn and finer sorts of cloth are manufactured in Poland in many branches than in Russia.

Let us turn to the second most important branch of capitalist production, the *coal industry.* We have already made mention of the strong concentration of this branch in Poland. Of the product extracted annually comes:

Coal in poods

	from 1 pit	from 1 shaft
in the South Russian district	678,000	240,000
In Poland	7,500,000	2,985,000
	(+1,006%)	(+1,144%)

(Here and below we compare the Polish coalfields with the South Russian fields in particular, because that is Russia's biggest reservoir and the most important for the future.)

A corresponding relationship is discovered when the quantity of production, the number of workers employed, and the steam power used are compared:

1890	Steampower	Workers	Production (in millions of poods)
Russia	6,701	30,077	213.4
South Russian district	5,856	25,167	183.2
Poland	10,497	8,692	150.8

Thus, while in Poland (1890), one worker raises 17,348 poods of coal a year, in Russia this comes to only 7,096 poods per worker and in the South Russian district in particular, 7,281 poods, approximately two and half times less than in Poland.

Steam power amounts to:

	for every 1,000 workers	for every shaft
Russia	223	8
South Russian district	233 (100%)	—
Poland	1,208 (+419%)	202

From 1890 to 1894, the amount of steampower in Polish mining rose by more than 50 per cent: from 10,497 to 15,934.

Of the other important branches of industry we want to single out the *sugar industry*.

Sugar-beet growing itself is carried on in a significantly more rational way in Poland than in the two Russian sugar production districts. For example, the average beet harvest per desyatin in the years 1882-1890 was:

Central Russia	73.2-125.3	berkovez
Southwestern Russia	80.1-114.4	berkovez
Poland	88.0-127.6	berkovez

In the year 1895:

Central Russia	51.1-117.4	berkovez
Southwestern Russia	90.0-121.2	berkovez
Poland	94.3-144.5	berkovez

Likewise, the quality of the Polish beet is much higher than the Russian. The sugar content of the juice and its purity are:

1890-91	Sugar content in juice	Purity
Southwestern district	13.49%	80.85%
Central district	13.63%	78.94%
Poland	14.81%	85.20%

The same superiority of Polish technology is shown by the higher yield of white sugar from the beet juice and the lower yield of molasses:

In 1881-82 — 1890-91 this was on average

	White sugar	Molasses
Central district	7.0- 9.47%	3.29-4.24%
Southwestern district	7.7-10.48%	3.60-4.31%
Poland	8.2-11.39%	1.53-2.28%

Finally, the utilization of processing by-products is far more intensive and more widespread in the Polish sugar industry than in the Russian. In 1890-91, of 182 factories in the central and southern districts, 10 with 125 osmosis devices conducted the extraction of sugar from molasses by osmosis; of 40 factories in Poland, 24 with 206 osmosis devices.

The above comparative analysis of the most important conditions of production shows that Polish industry is considerably better equipped than Russian and especially central Russian industry. Certainly it is a well-established fact that the Moscow district for its part exhibits an important advantage in the cotton industry, namely the abundance of water, while in this respect the Lodz district suffers from a tremendous shortage, as was mentioned. On the other hand, Poland lags behind in one of the most important branches of the economy — the iron industry — relative to the natural wealth of Russia, so that it must obtain part of the ore and likewise coke for its ironworks from the South Russian region. In addition, metal production in the Donets region is also much more concentrated than in Poland. It is furthermore true that Moscow is located much closer to the important market outlets for the textile industry — the eastern part of Russia and Asia — than Poland.

However, the advantages which we find in every branch on the Polish side — more capable labor power, cheaper fuel, higher technology in the production process and trade — could in our opinion outweigh numerous advantages of Russian industry. For all the cited factors have an invariant significance, indeed become more decisive in the competitive struggle with every passing day. How very much the significance of industry's distance from markets has already receded into the background, compared with its technical superiority, was recently proved by the amazing spread of the *German* market in England, and even in the English colonies. Within one and the same customs zone, of course, the outcome of competition in the market depends to still greater degree on the stage of development of production, i.e., on just those factors which *Polish* industry has on its side. This is corroborated by, among other things, the fact that the Polish iron industry, for example, despite the above-mentioned dearth of natural advantages, is mounting severe competition to the South Russian iron industry itself, and that the Polish iron industry is developing parallel to the South Russian industry, at the expense of every other district in the Empire. Aside from the Polish industrial sector, industry in St. Petersburg is also shaping up into a progressive and rather highly technically developed Russian industrial region, and it is a particularly favorable circumstance for Poland that in the most important markets it is in competition with the Moscow district — the most anachronistic industrial district in Russia, which is unique in the Empire in its long workday, low wages, truck system, barracks housing of the workforce, enormous stocks of raw materials, in short, its economic backwardness.

The coexistence of such diverse levels of production, as represented by the Polish and St. Petersburg industries on the one side and Moscow industry on the other, is possible only because of two circumstances: first, the size of the Russian market, in which all competitors can still find room for themselves, and second, the hot-house atmosphere created by the customs policy, which has made this enormous market the exclusive monopoly of domestic — Russian and Polish — entrepreneurs.

2.3 The Economic Ties Between Poland and Russia

After the foregoing, it is clear that — were only free competition to be decisive in the battle between Polish and Russian industry — the future of the former would be assured, at least to the degree that the capitalist development of the Russian Empire is granted a shorter or longer term by the general fate of the world economy.

However, we have already mentioned the other important factor which is of the greatest significance for the future of Polish capitalism—we mean *the economic policy of the Russian government.* It is all the more necessary to throw some light on precisely this factor, since the question (as is well known) stirred up so much dust a few years ago and one even comes across the notion that since the middle of the 1880s a real "era of persecution" has dawned for Polish industry.

Actually there are grounds enough to regard all assertions of this sort *a priori* as baseless. The best and last touchstone for all relevant government economic measures — the growth of industry in Poland up to the present moment, and still at the same impetuous tempo — sufficiently proves (it should seem) that all the uproar about Polish industry's approaching end was wrong. This growth is shown in the following striking table:

	1871	1885	1886	1887
▪ Output of total industry (branches not levied with excise)	44.4	134.8	137.8	164.5
▪ Total output of textile industry	18.1	66.7	81.4	88.9
○ Raw iron	1.4	2.5	2.8	3.7
○ Iron	0.9	4.2	4.6	3.8
○ Steel		2.4	3.1	3.0
○ Coal	12.6	109.3	120.0	121.1

	1888	1889	1890	1891
▪ Output of total industry (branches not levied with excise)	162.3	168.3	174.2	188.3
▪ Total output of textile industry	89.9	96.6	88.4	100.8
○ Raw iron	4.8	5.4	7.4	7.5
○ Iron	3.2	4.0	4.1	4.4
○ Steel	3.1	2.4	3.4	3.0
○ Coal	147.3	151.1	150.8	158.8

	1892	1893	1894	1895
▪ Output of total industry (branches not levied with excise)	228.3	—	—	—
▪ Total output of textile industry	113.4	—	—	—
○ Raw iron	9.0	9.9	10.7	11.3
○ Iron	3.7	3.5	3.8	3.6
○ Steel	4.0	5.4	6.2	7.9
○ Coal	176.0	192.1	202.4	221.8

▪ in millions of rubles   ○ in millions of poods

As can be seen from the above table, the growth in the seven-year period 1885-92 amounted to: 69 per cent in industry as a whole, 70 per cent in the textile industry (specifically, 40 per cent in cotton spinning and weaving, 77 per cent in the wool and cloth industry, 101 per cent in all other branches); in mining over the ten-year period 1885-95: 352 per cent for raw iron, 229 per cent for steel, 103 per cent for coal; only in the production of iron do we see a decline, of 14 per cent, as in recent times a vigorous development of steel production at the expense of iron production becomes observable in Poland and the South Russian district. Still more interesting than the growth during the latest period (1885-95) is the comparison of this decade with the previous period (1871-85), which is held to be the time of Poland's greatest economic prosperity. The increase, in absolute numbers, amounted to:

	Branches not levied with excise (in millions of rubles)	Textile Industry	Raw Iron	Iron and Steel (in millions of poods)	Coal
In the 14-year period 1871-1885	90.4	48.6	1.1	5.7	96.7
In the 7-year period 1885-1892	93.5	46.7	—	—	—
In the 10-year period 1885-1895	—	—	8.8	4.9	112.5

Thus, in view of the above figures, not only does speculation about the incipient decline of Polish industry rest on complete ignorance of the facts, but it is clear, on the contrary, that industry has grown more in the last seven- to ten-year period than in the preceding 14-year period. This becomes most clear when we calculate the growth in both periods *by year.* The average yearly growth in the later period was *greater* than in the preceding one, specifically: 107 per cent in industry as a whole, 90 per cent in the textile industry, 20 per cent in the production of iron and steel, of coal 63 per cent, of raw iron 1,020 per cent.

On the other hand, at the end of the first part of our work we also cited Polish industry's latest conquests in Russian and Asian markets into the 1890s. The body of Polish capitalism thus seems to exhibit not one symptom that would justify the claim that it is pining away from some internal malady; on the contrary, the much cried-over invalid grows and blooms "as splendidly as on the first day." But because the question was once raised and for years agitated public opinion in Poland, and also because it is interesting and important enough in itself, it seems appropriate to go into this question more fully and, through a thorough examination of the subject, to derive an explanation of what the situation is and can be with regard to the economic policy of the Russian government in general and toward Poland specifically.

It is characteristic of all the mentioned and quoted statements about the anti-Polish course that they are based exclusively on particular measures and decrees, sometimes in the sphere of customs policy, sometimes that of the railway fare system. But it is obvious that no real understanding of government policy can be reached by this road. For first of all, what is being referred to in the case at hand is a most extremely variable quantity: a tariff imposed today, a railway fare introduced today, will be lifted tomorrow. This is, in fact, what happened, for example with the differential tariff on raw cotton, which amounted to 15 kopeks in gold more on the Polish border than at the rest of Russia's borders. When it was introduced in 1887, a wail of lamentation went up among the Polish cotton-factory owners, and it was said that Polish industry had received its death blow. The differential tariff also played the leading role as proof that the "era of persecution" had begun, and it was denounced at every opportunity. But then this tariff difference was once again lifted in the year 1894, on the grounds of the Russian-German trade agreement, making way for a single tariff on cotton at all Russian borders. The same was the case with the differential tariff on coal and coke at the western border, which was frequently represented as a measure aimed directly against the Polish iron industry. But in 1894, this tariff was likewise reduced by half. In the same way, railway fares were changed in part every year, indeed sometimes even more frequently. Thus, the actual tariffs and fares *by themselves* do not provide a firm foothold from which to get an insight into Russia's economic policy.

To attain a thorough understanding of this policy, it is necessary to disregard particular measures for the present, to look deeper into the economic relations of Poland and Russia on the one hand and their political interests on the other, and to seek to derive from this the economic policy of the latter. Only by following the guideline thus obtained will it be possible to trace the particular measures of this policy back to their real significance.

THE INDUSTRIAL DEVELOPMENT OF POLAND

First of all, then, what is the nature of the economic ties between Poland and Russia? If one were to form an opinion under the immediate impression of the Lodz-Moscow entrepreneurs' battle, one would be inclined to assume that the Polish and Russian bourgeoisies form two completely separate camps, whose interests run directly counter to one another at every point and who both battle against each other using all available means. Such a notion would nonetheless be utterly wrong.

What precludes such a sharp difference in interests from the outset is the thoroughgoing *division of labor* which exists between the industries of these two countries. As we have seen, Poland is for Russia a source of supply for wool yarn, machines, coal, etc., etc., while Russia furnishes Poland with raw wool, raw iron, coke, and cotton.

Such a relationship already presupposes that the interests of some *Polish* manufacturers cohere with the interests of *Russian* raw materials producers, and that the interests of some Russian manufacturers cohere with those of Polish producers of half-finished goods. This is confirmed by abundant data. The producers of South Russian wool, the planters of central Asian cotton, exercise pressure on the railway fare system in their own interest to keep transport of their raw product to the Polish manufacturers as cheap as possible. Russian wool-weavers likewise seek to encourage the transport of Polish yarn to Russia as much as possible, etc., etc.

Furthermore, from the fact that the battle between the manufacturers and the producers of raw materials and half-finished goods is fought out in the sphere of the *common tariff policy* of the two countries, it follows that the battling parties from Poland would often unite with those from Russia in order to march hand-in-hand with the national enemy against their own brothers. The history of Russian-Polish industry provides examples in quantity. In the year 1850, for example, the Russian government, under the pressure of joint petitions by Polish and Russian wool-weavers, reduced the tariff rate on wool yarn. But hardly had this happened when Polish and Russian spinners, in touching accord, beseiged the government to again push up the tariff rate on yarn, which happened in 1867. Beginning in 1882, the government was solicited by the machine producers to increase the tariff on foreign machinery. "In this connection the initiative was that of the Riga manufacturers, who were followed by the others in *Warsaw,* Kiev, Kharkov, and Odessa with great unanimity." However, when the government had obeyed this wish and increased the tariffs on machinery, a storm of petitions arose from the property owners, again from all over the Empire without differentiation, against the increased price of agricultural machinery.

Just these two examples give us a quite different picture of the relationship between the Polish and Russian bourgeoisies, in their collective just as in their competitive endeavors. Neither of the two national capitalist classes appears from the inside as a closed phalanx, but on the contrary are fissured, torn by conflicts of interest, split by rivalries. Yet, on the other hand, their different groups, unmindful of the national quarrel, reach out their hands to one another in order to deal their own countrymen an opportune blow to the wallet in the glorious prize-fight for profits. Thus, it is not national but capitalist parties that are found opposed on the industrial chessboard, not Poles and Russians, but spinners and weavers, machine producers and landowners, and on the flags waving over the combatants one sees not the one- and two-headed eagles, but only the international emblem of capitalism. Finally, the government unexpectedly appears in the strange role of an indulgent mother, who impartially hugs all her profit-making children to her broad bosom, even though they are constantly squabbling with each other, and seeks to appease now the one, now the other, at the expense of the consumers.

The above phenomena recur countless times in the history of Polish and Russian industry, and are of such decisive importance for the question under consideration here that it is well worthwhile to give a few more typical cases as examples. It is, for example, most highly instructive to observe how the two main opponents — the entrepreneurs of the Lodz and Moscow districts —whom one would be inclined to accept as representatives of the interests of, respectively, the Polish and Russian bourgeoisies as a whole, try at every opportunity to trip up the other industrial districts of their own countries. Thus, the Lodz cotton manufacturers, in their above-mentioned polemic, seek to turn the jealousy of the Moscow manufacturers away from themselves and toward the old Polish wool industry district of Bialystock. "If one can speak of a competition, then far more dangerous to Moscow is Bialystock and its district," they assure their adversaries. Meanwhile, these same Lodz entrepreneurs most humbly and obediently denounce their blood-brothers of the Sosnowiec district to the Russian government, pointing to the fact that in the latter a full third of the workforce are *German* subjects, while in the Lodz district — thank God — only 8 per cent.

No less brotherly sentiment is displayed by the Moscow capitalists when they come to speak of the affairs of their comrades in the other Russian industrial districts. So we hear them bewail the result of a plan for the regulation of waterways worked out by the Ministry of Transport: "The small expenditures, just like those of many millions, are allotted exclusively for Russia's western and southern zone. The whole central region of Russia has been almost entirely forgotten. This region, this neglected center of Russia, key Russian gubernias, is relatively poor in waterways," and so forth in the same weepy tone. Here the jealousy of the Moscow capitalists gushes forth with impartiality and true internationalism against all other industrial districts in the Empire without distinction, against Poland and the Volga region, against the Baltic Sea provinces and the Dnieper district.

The following example shows how elastic the notion of national solidarity and the "Fatherland" can be for the Polish capitalists under certain circumstances. In the year 1887, the large Warsaw steel factory was relocated to the Yekaterinoslav gubernia in South Russia, to be nearer to sources of supply of raw iron and coke. Two years later, its owners — Polish capitalists — together with the English, Belgians, Russians, etc., who hold the South Russian iron district under their dominion, sent a most humble and obedient petition to the government in which they complain about the advantages of the *Polish* iron industry and the competition from that quarter, and beg for an increased railway fare rate on Polish iron for the protection of the "Fatherland's" — i.e., this time South Russia's — industry.

Last, a classic example of this situation was provided in recent years by the question of the railway fare rates for grain. In 1889 new, strongly differential rates were introduced for grain as part of the general regulation of the Empire's fare system, to facilitate exports from the gubernias lying deep in inner Russia to other countries. However, the result was that masses of grain and flour from the inner city regions, particularly the Volga district, were sent to the regions lying near the border, thus bringing on a rapid fall in the price of grain in the southern provinces on the Black Sea, in the Baltic provinces, and finally in Poland. Injured in their most virtuous sentiments, the landowners in all these parts of the Empire cried bloody murder, most of all the Polish landowners who in the beginning tried to take this opportunity to again step forward in the name of all Poland, oppressed by cheap bread. Yet, hardly was their national defense crowned by success and the execrated fare partially annulled in the beginning of 1894, when a group of Polish entrepreneurs and merchants entreated the Railway Department in St. Petersburg, *by telegram*, to maintain the earlier fare rate in order, as they put it, not to make bread more costly for the people. The picture thus shifted from moment to moment, and from a fight between two national parties the grain tariff question turned into a dispute between the landed proprietors and the industrialists in Poland. Here the latter marched together with the Russian landowners of the central gubernias, while the Polish landowners took the field jointly with the Russian landowners of all the border districts.

This motley grouping of interests was particularly evident in the deliberations on grain tariffs in St. Petersburg in October 1896. On the one side stood the representatives of the Volga district, whose case, as we have seen, was at the same time that of the Polish industrialists; on the other side, the landed proprietors of Livland, Vitebsk, Odessa, the Polish landowners, and also, what is most interesting, the landowners of the Moscow district. Here Poles and Muscovites appeared on the best of terms, and the Polish landowners and millers declared themselves in full agreement with the program of Prince Shcherbatov, the chairman of the Moscow Agricultural Society. Almost as if to underline the conflict of interests between industry and agriculture in Poland itself, on the other hand, Chairman Maximov of the Polish representatives (among others) objected: If Poland were permitted to sell its factory products in inner Russia unhindered, then it would be highly inconsistent to forbid access to Poland to agricultural products from inner Russia.

May it appear as proven after the above examples, which we do not want to pile too high, that the interests of the Polish and Russian entrepreneur groups absolutely do not contradict each other on all points — that, much more, they continually mesh together. But also, on the whole, Polish industry is tied up with several important sections of the Russian bourgeoisie by a solidarity of interests, above all with the two most important factors of economic life: the institutions of transport and credit and trade. It is obvious that the development of Polish industry and, together with this, of the Polish market in Russia is directly in the interests of the Russian credit, factoring, and railway corporations. To again pull out only two from the abundance of striking examples: the administration of the Russian railway line Rjasan-Ural turned to the Warsaw entrepreneurs in the fall of 1894 with the offer to hand over space in all its stations, free of charge, so that the Polish factory owners could have permanent displays of goods there to encourage Poland's market in the Volga region. Thus, while the Moscow factory owners wanted to do battle with their Polish competitors over every market in Russia, the Russian railway corporations invited this same Polish competition to forge ahead with its goods as deeply as possible into inner Russia.

Another characteristic case took place recently as a result of the new tariff on cotton. So long as the above-mentioned difference in customs rates was maintained on the western border, the Lodz factory owners, in order to get around the troublesome tariff, got their cotton via Libau and Odessa, i.e., by means of Russian railroads. When the customs difference was annulled in 1894, cotton transport returned to the old land routes: Bremen-Alexandrovo and Triest-Granica, thus to German and Austrian railways. Now the latter used this opportunity to set very low freight rates for cotton and so to monopolize this transport for themselves at the expense of the Odessa-Lodz line. The loss of transport, however, hit the Russian railways hard, and so the St. Petersburg railway department has recently turned to the Lodz factory owners with the question of how much to decrease the freight rates on the Russian lines so that cotton transport would once more go via Odessa. The Lodz factory owners dictated a rate decrease of 30 per cent. Likewise the Russian banks, in their own interest, are promoting Polish sales in Russia whenever possible. Once again national borders clash with capitalist interests, and what the national banner should keep asunder is intimately bound together by capitalist interest.

Finally, there is also another area in which the most touching harmony of interests rules between the whole Polish and the whole Russian bourgeoisie, where they are of one heart and soul: the jealous guarding of the profits sought in the domestic market from foreign competition. One can encounter in one section of the Western European press the view that the Polish entrepreneurs are greater believers in free trade than the Russian. Nothing could be more mistaken. In the deep conviction that Russian and Polish workers were created solely to produce surplus value for them, Polish and Russian consumers to assist the realization of surplus value, the Russian government to fend off any invasion of foreign competition into this holy Empire — in this conviction the Polish entrepreneurs are just as firm and unshakable as the Russians. When it comes to taking a stand in defense of these "fundamental rights" of the capitalist constitution vis-a-vis the government, then the Lodz and Moscow factory owners, still bearing the bruises they just inflicted on each other, go shoulder to shoulder into battle. In 1888, one year after the two adversaries — as was mentioned — had sent a petition to the government in which they most sharply fought each other on the question of domestic competition, the Moscow entrepreneurs submitted a series of "most humble and obedient" petitions in regard to tariff policy: on increasing the entry tariffs for products of the textile industry, on reimbursing tariffs paid on raw materials when exported by manufacturers to foreign countries, etc. — all demands which had also freqeuntly been made now as well as previously by the Lodz manufacturers. With reason, then, the organ of the large Polish industrialists, in discussing this action by the Moscow entrepreneurs, wrote that while much used to be said about the conflict of interests between the two industrial districts, now this petition shows that there is also a community of interests between the two, and indeed on the most important questions.

The same harmony is evident when it comes to defending the monopoly in profits against the "Germans." The Moscow factory owners — as was shown — saw in the strong representation of German elements in the Polish bourgeoisie a tempting pretext to lend their calico and fustian interests a becomingly patriotic look in the battle against Lodz. When they called the government to a crusade against the Germans on the Vistula river, they believed that they were striking the Polish bourgeoisie right in the heart.

THE INDUSTRIAL DEVELOPMENT OF POLAND

When, however, the government issued its well known ukase in 1887, and when, because of this ukase, there was talk on many sides of an era of persecution against the Polish bourgeoisie, then it turned out that the Polish bourgeoisie expressed their dissatisfaction on quite unexpected grounds: namely, for them the Russian government's anti-German measures were not nearly energetic and radical enough. For, as they expressed it, "The government's decree of two years ago concerning language examinations for foreigners brought about an advantageous change, in that it opened up a sphere of action for native forces...Correspondents from Lodz and inhabitants there have already reported a certain improvement in this situation *although it is still far from what it could and should be.*"

We have reviewed the many-sided coherence of interests between the Polish and Russian bourgeoisies. The picture which emerges is absolutely different from that which might be gotten under the immediate impression of Lodz and Moscow's battle cries. On countless, extremely important questions, the Polish and the Russian bourgeoisies are bound together in a solidarity of interests, in particular groups as much as on the whole. What has created this community of interests is, first, the division of labor in production, which in many ways unified the two into a single productive mechanism; second, still more important, the common tariff borders, which breed solidarity against the outside and merge the entire Polish-Russian bourgeosie — from the standpoint of the market — into a "national" capitalist class. Finally, the common market, which bred the important, reciprocal dependency between Polish production on the one side and Russian transport on the other. And, as is generally known, this fusion of Russian and Polish economic interests advances every day. This is also, in part, a direct result of the general direction of current Russian tariff policy, which in effect closes the way into Russia to not only foreign manufactured goods but also foreign raw materials, and creates domestic raw materials production — in which task it does not shy away from the greatest sacrifices out of the pockets of Russian and Polish consumers and taxpayers.

Forced by prohibitive tariffs, Polish industry is changing gradually from the use of German coke and iron ore over to that of Donets, from American and Indian to central Asian cotton, from Saxon and Silesian to South Russian wool. The reciprocal dependency of Polish and Russian production as a whole grows to the same degree, and the interests of ever newer circles of the Russian bourgeoisie become tied to the weal and woe of Polish industry.

Certainly just as much enmity, competition, and rivalry grow out of these same relations between the Polish and Russian bourgeoisies. The same industrial division of labor, the common tariff boundaries, and the common markets turn the most varied groups within the bourgeoisie into enemies, and every particular solidarity of interests corresponds to a conflict of interests. As the examples have shown us, land ownership opposes industry, production opposes transport, and within each of these groups one district opposes the others and every individual capitalist opposes all the others. But what we glimpse here is a typical picture of capitalist economy, as it puts forth its blossoms in every country. It is the fundamental law of this form of production: *bellum omnium contra omnes* (a war of all against all), which is expressed here and which has nothing to do with national contradictions and borders, indeed, on the contrary, ceaselessly wipes away these contradictions and borders within the capitalist class.

Certainly, if the conflicts of economic interests coincide with national borders within one and the same state, this creates a broad basis, circumstances permitting, for national aspirations. This can only be the case, however, insofar as the enemy nationalities represent different, inherently antagonistic *forms of production;* if, for example, one country represents small business, the other large industry, one natural economy, the other money economy. In the given case, however, the situation is totally different, since Poland and Russia have gone through a *combined* development from a natural to a money economy and from small to large industry. Their antagonism, when and where it comes to light, arises not from the dissimilarity but rather the homogeneity of economic structure, and exhibits the characteristics of all capitalist *competitive battles* within one and the same economic mechanism.

The competitive Lodz-Moscow dispute is nothing but a fragment of this general war. Superficially puffed up to Poland's national duel with Russia in the economic battlefield, this dispute in its fundamentals reduces itself to an argument between the Lodz fustian barons and the Moscow calico kings. Following international custom, the two capitalist parties sought first to cover over the trivial cotton object of contention with an ideological national cloak and then to bang the drum as loudly as though their very necks were at stake.

Nonetheless, in reality neither one nor the other party represents the interests of the whole Polish and Russian bourgeoisies — on the contrary, both have countless opponents among their own countrymen — nor is the fiery competitive battle over domestic markets decisive to or characteristic of the relationship of the disputants. Their rivalry over the domestic markets is contradicted by their solidarity of interests on a whole series of other vital capitalist issues.

In the entire capitalist development of Poland and Russia, which proceeds from an ever stronger bond between the production and exchange of the two countries, the Lodz-Moscow cotton dispute plays an infinitesimally tiny role—if one is not led astray by the behavior of the squabbling entrepreneurs and keeps the wider perspective of the whole capitalist chessboard in view.

Only now, from the basis of these material interests, can the economic policy of the Russian government be evaluated and explained. Russia's main concern since the 1870s, as is well enough known, is the rearing of capitalism. To this end, the prohibitive tariff policy is followed, the hot-house atmosphere of monopoly prices and profits created in the Empire, the costly means of transport built, subsidies and premiums awarded to "needy" capitalists, etc., etc. From this standpoint, the development of capitalism in Poland (just as in other parts of the Empire) appears as partial realization of the government's own program, its retrogression as a thwarting of this program. But still more important than the Russian government's own economic designs are the objective tendencies of the Russian economy. The bourgeoisie, reared by the government, already plays a significant role in Russia. The government must now seriously reckon with the bourgeoisie's interests, but also wants to carry through its own. The interests of the Russian bourgeoisie, however, are — as was shown — interwoven with those of the Polish bourgeoisie in the most diverse ways. There is no point at which Polish industry could be dealt a serious and lasting body blow without at the same time grievously wounding the vital interests of this or that group of the Russian bourgeoisie.

The notion that Russia is destroying or could destroy Polish capitalism assumes that Russian economic policy could be made the exclusive tool of the interests of the handful of Moscow calico manufacturers, an assumption based on a misunderstanding of the nature of the bourgeoisie just as much as of the nature of a capitalist government. Given the splits and contradiction of interests within the capitalist class, the government can represent the interests of the latter only *as a whole;* it cannot continually take the standpoint of any particular group of the bourgeoisie without being forced away from this standpoint again by the opposition of the other groups. Even the Russian government — although absolute — is no exception to this rule. For even in Russia the bourgeoisie is a political tool of the government only to the extent that the government is the tool of the bourgeoisie's economic interests. Were the absolutist Russian government to make itself exclusively the lawyer for the Moscow cotton interests and trample on Polish and therefore Russian capitalist interests for this purpose, then it could not help but call for the strong bourgeois opposition to the government in Russia itself. The end result of such a policy could even be efforts by the Russian and Polish bourgeoisies for a reform government which would know how to safeguard their interests as a whole better than the existing regime. Thus, from this side, the question of the future of Polish capitalism is decided: *were it to be injured by the Russian government, the government's efforts would fall to pieces through the violent opposition of the bourgeoisie in Russia and Poland.*

From this standpoint we can also reduce the whole question of the alleged persecution of Polish industry to its true value. All the measures which are usually introduced as proof of Russian anti-Polish economic policy have *one* common characteristic: namely, they are all directed to keeping Polish industry from the use of foreign raw materials and to the purchase of Russian raw materials. This was the case with the differential tariffs on cotton, on coal, on raw iron. All these measures were proclaimed not for the advantage of Russian industries competing with Poland and not with the purpose of destroying Polish industry, but to the advantage of the Russian raw materials production tied to Polish industry and with the purpose of achieving *a particular configuration* of Polish industry. Precisely the same Russian interests that called forth these measures would form the greatest obstacle to a government policy directed at the destruction of Polish industry.

Yet from the same necessity of satisfying all the so very contradictory interests of the different groups of the bourgeoisie, there arises for the government the necessity of moving in an increasing zig-zag course in its economic policy. All laws of the capitalist method of production are merely "laws of gravity," i.e., laws which do not move in a straight line on the shortest route, but on the contrary proceed with constant deflections in contrary directions. The government's general policy of promoting capitalism, correspondingly, can only be realized as it favors now this capitalist faction, now that. The examples of Russian customs and railway policy given above showed crudely the zig-zag course of the Russian government, which at one time protects manufacture at the expense of semi-finished manufacture, at another time takes care of the latter at the expense of the former, at one time patronizes coal mining over iron works, at another time patronizes the iron works at the "coal interests' " expense, favoring sometimes the landowners, sometimes the industrialists. This characteristic of the government's economic policy also means that it can temporarily and on various questions deeply offend one or another *Polish* capitalist group; this is not only not impossible, but follows directly, necessarily from the nature of the situation. The differential railway tariff for grain, etc. was of this type.

However, if all these temporary and one-sided phenomena were torn out of their complicated economic context and puffed up into a doctrine of Russia's anti-Polish economic conspiracy, then what is involved is a complete lack of perspective and overview of the totality of this policy. In the same way, the exaggeration of the skirmish between Lodz fustian and Moscow calico into a deep gulf between the interests of Polish and Russian capitalism reveals the lack of an overview of the totality of the capitalist community of interest. There can be no doubt that the Moscow district, more than any other, has up until now enjoyed particularly loving care from the government, expressed in gifts of every sort. This policy, however, is merely the concrete expression of the encouragement of Russian capitalism in general, since the central district (where nearly a third of the Empire's industry and approximately two-thirds the textile industry, by value, is concentrated) forms its main branch. The cost of this favoritism toward the Muscovites has not, however, been borne so much by the other industrial districts of the Empire, which in most cases (for example, the customs policy), on the contrary, also benefit, but much more by the other branches of the economy, above all agriculture. In fact, the enmity between the Russian landowners and the Moscow industrialists is much more lasting and bitter than that between Moscow and Lodz. An interesting spotlight on the alleged "national" policy of the Russian government, on the other hand, is thrown by the well-known fact that it is the southern coal and iron region which is most coddled and absolutely overwhelmed with patronage — at the expense of the Russian metal industry in the Urals as well as the Moscow industrial interests —, a region whose exploitation is in the main in foreign hands: Belgian and English capitalists.

It is as superficial as it is erroneous to ascribe a national (in the ethnographic sense), "Great Russian" economic policy to the Russian government. Such a policy exists only in the imagination of the reporter led astray by external appearances. In fact, the Czarist government — just as any other in the present day — maintains not a national but a class policy; it differentiates not between *Polish* and *Russian* enterprises, but only between those that "establish" or "own" and those that labor.

2.4 Russia's Political Interests in Poland

Although the economic relations between Russia and Poland treated above unquestionably represent the leading feature in the shape of Russia's economic policy toward Poland, it would nevertheless be one-sided to see this policy as determined simply and solely by the interests of the Russian bourgeoisie. For the present, the absolutist government of Russia is more able than that of any other country to carry through its own political interests, its sovereign interests, as well. In this connection, however, the historic state of affairs between the Russian government and Polish industry has formed a unique relationship. It is easy to see that absolutism's interests in terms of Poland are based above all on maintaining and fortifying the annexation. Since the Vienna Congress, Russia's special attention has been directed to tenaciously suppressing all traces of national opposition in Poland, particularly that of the social class which is the pillar of the opposition, the nobility. In this endeavor Russian absolutism saw in the industrial bourgeoisie of Poland a desirable ally. To bind Poland to Russia through material interests, and to create a counterweight to the nationalist ferment of the nobility in a capitalist class arisen under the very wing of the Russian eagle, a class disposed toward servility not through any tradition of a national past but through an interest in its future — this was the aim of Russian policy, which it followed with its usual iron consistency. It must be admitted that the Russian government did not err in its choice of means, and that it had correctly sensed the nature of the Polish bourgeoisie. Hardly had manufacture sprouted in Poland, hardly had it tasted the honey of the Russian market, when the Polish entrepreneurs felt themselves ready for their historic mission: to serve as the support in Poland for the Russian annexation. Already in 1826, the Polish Finance Minister Drucki-Lubecki was delegated to St. Petersburg with the most humble entreaty to completely abolish the customs border between Russia and Poland, "since indeed the two countries form one whole and Poland belongs to Russia." In this declaration, the entire political program of the Polish bourgeoisie was concisely enunciated: the complete renunciation of national freedom in exchange for the mess of pottage of the Russian market. Since that time, the Russian government has never ceased supporting the Polish bourgeoisie. We have cited the long list of laws which have been issued since the 1820s to aid industrial colonization of Poland and the development of manufacture, the "iron fund" for the subsidy of industry, the establishment of the Polish Bank, endowed with every conceivable privilege, etc., etc.

This policy was most energetically maintained in the later period; even in the time of Nicholas I we see the Russian government issue new decrees to the same effect. Nothing was neglected which might transform the noble, rebellious Pole into a capitalist, tame Pole. And the Polish bourgeoisie showed that it possesses a grateful heart, for it has never ceased to thwart and betray national stirrings in Poland with all its might; its disgraceful conduct in the Polish uprisings supplies sufficient evidence of this fact. The most important milestone of this tendency in Russian policy was the abolition of the Russian-Polish customs border in 1851. A historian intimate with the pertinent archives of the Russian government and the best authority on the history of Russian customs tariffs, the Russian Lodyshenki, wrote on this subject:

"The lifting of the customs line between the Empire and the Kingdom was primarily the result of *motives of a political character*. As is well known, an intellectual ferment of partly *national* and partly socialist character began in Europe in the 1840s. This ferment, in which the population of Russian Poland also participated, disturbed the Russian government up to a certain point and moved it to seek out ways to *unite Poland with Russia as firmly as possible*. One of the main factors which hindered the drawing together of the two countries was their economic separation." Thus to eliminate this "separation," to fetter Poland to Russia by the material interests of its bourgeoisie, the customs border was abolished. The Russian government still holds to the same standpoint today, and still greets the growing Polish market in Russia as the chain which most tightly shackles the annexed country to Russia. Thus, Mendeleyev wrote in his preface to the official report on Russian industry to the Chicago World's Fair in 1893: "The products of this and many other Polish factories find a constantly growing market all over Russia. Through the competition of this industrial district with the Moscow district, the basic goal of Russia's protectionist policy was achieved on the one hand and, on the other, the assimilation of Poland with Russia, which is appropriate to the peaceable outlook of the Russian people (read: the Russian government)."

This special role which the Polish bourgeoisie plays toward the Russian government as the bulwark of the annexation also is important in explaining the main point under question, i.e., the future of Polish capitalism. It requires, in fact, an enormous dose of naiveté to impute that the Russian government, which has given itself precisely the task of cultivating capitalism in Poland and has for more than half a century used all the means at its disposal to do so, now intends to demolish that same capitalism, force the Polish bourgeoisie over to the opposition, and thus wantonly destroy its own handiwork. And indeed, solely out of love for the Moscow entrepreneurs, to whose complaints and lamentations the Russian government has turned a deaf ear for half a century! Unfortunately, the Russian government knows better how to protect its ruling interests. What these interests are in regard to Poland we know from the mouths of its representatives: "the peaceable assimilation" of Poland with Russia, i.e., the strengthening of its rule in Poland at any price. This declaration was made in 1893, long after the presumed new course of Russian policy was supposed to have begun.

The best evidence of our interpretation is provided by the recent history of Russia's relations with *Finland*. Here we find on a small scale an exact repetition of Russia's earlier policy in Poland. Finland, at present, remains cut off from the Czarist Empire by a customs border and maintains an independent customs policy toward foreign countries much more liberal than Russia's. Finnish industry is now enjoying all the advantages that have already helped Polish industry to blossom. Likewise Finnish products, particularly those of the metal industry, have found access to Russia thanks to, among other things, lower customs at the Russo-Finnish border than at Russia's other borders, and is now giving Russia's domestic industry fierce competition. The Russian entrepreneurs, to whom this is a thorn in the side, have, of course, not neglected to set in motion a "most humble and obedient" campaign to protect the "Fatherland's" industries against "foreign" rivals — exactly like the campaign against Poland. The government has, under this pressure, likewise twice raised the tariffs against Finland as an economically foreign region, because of its independent customs policy, in 1885 and 1897.

If the Russian government were now to make the interests of this or that group of entrepreneurs the consistent plumbline for its economic policy toward the non-Russian-speaking sections of the Empire, then it would consequently have had to continue along the road to cutting Finland off from Russia with a Chinese wall. But precisely the opposite is in fact the case. The government has already ordered *the total lifting of the Russian-Finnish customs border* for the year 1903 and the absorption of Finland into the imperial Russian customs zone. Thus will the "Fatherland's" industries be freed of uninhibited "foreign" competition. And if this has not happened even sooner, it is not consideration for the lamentations of the Russian mill-owners which is responsible, but the trade agreement with Germany, through which the Czarist Empire has bound itself for a number of years. It is clear that the impending reform means the beginning of the end of Finnish independence in *political* terms, even if it proceeds first toward demolishing its economic independence. Here we have before us once more a portion of the general policy of Czarism, which passes over all particular interests in order to spiritually level the various parts of the Empire through the system of Russification on the one hand, and, on the other, to give the unity of the Empire a firm material frame by this economic welding process, and to press the whole thing together in the iron clamps of absolute power — a policy which we have already become acquainted with in Poland.

Of course not everything in the world goes according to the wishes of the rulers. While the Russian government economically incorporates Poland into the Empire and cultivates capitalism as the "antidote" to national opposition, at the same time it raises up a new social class in Poland — the industrial proletariat — a class which is forced by its situation to become the most serious opponent of the absolutist regime. And if the proletariat's opposition cannot have a national character, so it can under the circumstances be even more effective, in that it will logically answer the solidarity of the Polish and Russian bourgeoisie with the political solidarity of the Polish and Russian proletariat. But this distant consequence of its policy cannot divert the Russian government from its present course; for the time being, it sees in the capitalist development of Poland only the class of the bourgeoisie. As long as Russia seeks to maintain its rule over Poland in this way, the riotous bloom of industry in Poland will remain inscribed in the program of the government. Thus, those who await a government policy directed toward the economic separation of Poland take for future phenomena that which belongs to the past, and their insufficient knowledge of history for deeper insight into the future.

2.5 Russia's Economic Interests in the Orient

Of eminent significance for the question we are dealing with, finally, is the new direction in Russian foreign economic policy which has become evident in the last ten years. Up until that time, Russia's efforts were directed to satisfying its needs for manufactured goods and raw materials through its own production and emancipating itself from foreign imports. Today, its efforts go further; today, Russia wants to venture out into the world market and challenge the other capitalist nations on foreign ground. To be sure, this tendency does not stem from the Russian bourgeoisie; because of the peculiar economic-political development of Russia, politics frequently grasps the initiative of economic progress out of its own interests.

While industry in most capitalist countries, to the extent that the boundaries of the internal market are too narrow, pushes the government to acquire new markets by conquest or treaty, in Russia, on the contrary, Czarist policy sees in industrial exports a means of bringing the countries of Asia chosen as poli⁺ al booty into, first, economic dependence on Russia. Therefore, while the Russian industrialists for the most part do not lift a finger to win a place in the world market, the government spurs them incessantly in this direction. Everything has been used to impart energy and a thirst for exports: exhortations, invitations, expeditions to investigate new market areas, the construction of colossal railways such as the Siberian and East Chinese, rebates on customs and taxes on exported goods, finally, direct subsidies to this end. The countries first in consideration here are: China, Persia, Central Asia, and the Balkan states. In 1892, an expedition under the direction of Professor Pozdneev, which was to serve scientific as well as commercial ends, was sent to *Mongolia*. Even earlier the Russians had introduced the post-wagon system there, which was also run by them. In the following year, the official of the Finance Ministry, Tomara, was sent to *Persia* to investigate the trade situation there and, particularly important, the reconstruction of the Persian port of Enseli was begun in order to support Russian trade. In the same year, the Finance Ministry worked out a draft regarding the improvement of the routes from the Russian border to Teheran, Tauris, and Meschhed and the establishment of a Russian bank in Persia. To monopolize the market in East Siberia for its own merchants and knock the English out of the field, Russia decided to abolish the free port on the Amur river and in the port of Vladivostok, which has extended to all goods except those on which an excise had been levied in Russia. However, the most important measure, by which the government hoped to give a leg up to Russian trade in Central Asia, was the costly construction of the Trans-Caspian railway.

No less, or more correctly, even more attention did Russia direct toward China. A short time ago, China's trade with foreign countries was taken care of by German, French, and some English banks. Therefore, in 1896, the Russian government hurried to found a Russian bank in Shanghai. "One task of the bank," wrote the organ of the Russian Finance Ministry at the time, "is to consolidate Russia's economic influence in China and to thereby create a counterweight to the influence of other European nations. From this standpoint it is particularly important that the bank try to draw as close to the Chinese government as possible, that it collect taxes in China, undertake operations which will bring it into contact with the Chinese treasury, pay interest on the Chinese state debt," etc. The other Russian measures, for example the construction of the East Chinese railway, are well enough known.

The result of these efforts so far was recently officially examined and has shown itself to be an almost total fiasco. In every country where the government wanted to set it up, the Russian market would have had to overcome stiff competition from German, French, but above all English industry, and the Russian entrepreneurs had not yet shown themselves to have sufficiently grown to the part. Russia was no match for other nations even in its own national territory in East Siberia, as long as it had to face them in free competition. Imports in the most important Siberian port, Vladivostok, amounted to:

	In thousands of rubles	
	from Russia	from foreign countries
1887	2,016	3,725
1888	2,121	3,763
1889	2,385	3,325

A consequence of this state of affairs was the above-mentioned decision by Russia to take East Siberia into the Empire's tariff zone.

Russian exports to *China* are likewise hardly worth mention in comparison to those of other nations. Out of total imports of nearly 330 million rubles, Russia participated with only approximately 4.5 million:

thousands of rubles	
1891	4,896
1892	4,782
1893	4,087
1894	4,488

A similar picture has been provided by the uproar about trade with *central Asia*. The Trans-Caspian railway built by Russia, on which such great hopes were set, proved itself to be a really first-rate trade route — for the English, who now have obtained a way of getting around the high transit duty in

Afghanistan. Russian exports to the Trans-Caspian, Khiva, Bukhara, and Turkestan have, after a brief upswing, begun to sink again in the last few years. Of the most important articles registered, the following were transported:

Year	1888	1889	1890	1891	1892	1893
	thousands of rubles					
Total	1,141	1,296	1,685	2,922	2,102	1,854
Products of textile industry	201	245	541	671	397	538
Sugar	422	457	531	1,048	516	510

English imports from India, on the contrary, grew rapidly during the same period thanks to the Russian railway, as has been officially confirmed from the Russian side. Bukhara, for example, received from the four main stations on this line:

	1888	1889	1890	1891	1892	1893	Total
	In thousands of poods						
Russian products	572	1,176	1,863	923	267	244	5,045
English products	1,160	4,209	8,516	12,761	4,443	16,154	47,243

Russia's exports to *Afghanistan* are in just as bad a way. Imports of products of the Russian textile industry amounted to 163,245 poods in 1888-1890 (25 months), 10,000 poods in 1893 (12 months), that is, approximately eight times less per year.

Russian trade *in Persia* has succeeded the best, relatively. Russian cotton products make up approximately 30 per cent of Persian consumption, and imports of these products amount to 48,000 poods per year in 1887-1890, 73,000 poods per year in 1891-1894.

In the northern provinces of Gilan and Masenderan, the Russian textile industry has almost supplanted the English, but, in total Persian imports, Russia — according to official evidence — plays a very small role for the meantime. This despite the fact that the Russian industry finds itself in the most advantageous situation, since the Persians and Armenians living in the Caucasus, carrying on trade at their own risk, serve Russian industry as the most suitable agents, while the merchants of other nations must take recourse to business on commission, and that only in Persia's larger cities.

The total picture of Russia's exports to its most important Asian markets looks as follows:

1894	to Persia	to China	to Central Asia
	In millions of rubles		
Total	12	4.5	3.8
Food	7.5	0.1	1.7
Manufactured goods	3.5	3.4	0.4
Raw materials and half-finished goods	—	0.7	0.9

We see that the Russian government's program in Asia is still far from being realized, and that, in any case, the result attained corresponds in no way to the amount of effort made in this direction. It would be an error to trace this back to the technological backwardness of Russian industry alone. Certainly Russia is behind other industrial states in this regard, in a whole series of important branches of industry — such as the metal and wool industries, etc. — and, in order to be able to take up the competitive battle successfully on the world market, it would have to unconditionally improve its methods of production. But there is a further and no less important factor involved, which has largely frustrated the government's plans in Asia up until now. For even where Russian industry could have easily won a victory over the English, according to the competent testimony of individual researchers and even the British consuls in Persia — for example in the production of lower grades of cotton cloth — the Russian industrialists up until now have not been able to go very far.

The reason is the entire habitat of the Russian and especially the Moscow entrepreneurs, which was formed by years of Russia's prohibitive tariff policy. Pampered by the government with all sorts of gifts and patronage, spoiled by enormous monopoly profits, spoiled further by a colossal domestic market and the immunity from outside competition, the Moscow entrepreneurs felt neither the desire nor the need to expose themselves to the rough weather of the world market and content themselves with normal profits. It is, so to speak, profit-hypertrophy which makes the Muscovites so sluggish and apathetic in the search for possible new markets; they see foreign trade as, at most, a means to either pocket higher export subsidies or to get a huckster's one-time profit by fraudulent goods deliveries and the clumsiest cheating. If neither the one nor the other is in the offing, then the Moscow manufacturer answers the orders that might pour in from outside with stubborn silence.

This method of doing business is clearly shown in connection with Asia. Thus, for example, the Russian calico, massively imported to Bukhara and Khiva in 1890 and 1891, was manufactured in such a way that the Moslems could have used it much less for clothing than for dyeing New Year's eggs. In subsequent years, the population understandably turned back to English products, and this, more than the cholera epidemic and the bad harvest, brought about the precipitous fall in Russian imports in the years 1892 and 1893. Just as telling is the story of the sugar trade with Asia. So long as the excise was rebated on the export of sugar, these exports went rapidly to Persia and Bukhara; when the rebates were suspended, the business once more seemed pointless to the Russians, and exports sank suddenly from 1,047,996 poods in 1891 to 516,021 poods in 1892 and 150,128 in 1893. Another interesting side of the Muscovites' commercial spirit is revealed in their trade with Siberia, where they managed to first send out travelers with samples to win orders, then afterwards declined to fill these orders. Finally, the Muscovites' energy comes to the fore most glaringly in their business with China; approached from there with requests for the establishment of trade relations, they retorted to this importunate demand with silence.

After exhaustive examination of the outcome of Russia's Asiatic trade, the organ of the Finance Ministry likewise came to the following conclusion: "The characteristic traits of the non-commercial Slavic (meaning here: Russian) race and the absolute apathy and indolence of the Moscow entrepreneurs are expressed as crudely as they are completely in our trade with Central Asia." The causes of the failure of the Russian market in Asia are formulated in almost the same words by other papers of different viewpoints — the "Novosti," "Novoe Vremya," "St. Petersburg News," among others. And recently, the organ of the Finance Ministry happened to speak once again on the same theme: "Only Persia," it wrote in January 1897, "can be called a market for the products of our cotton industry; the attempts to conquer the Chinese and Central Asian markets for ourselves can so far not be viewed as successful, and what is responsible is in part our inability to adjust to the demands and customs of the customers, but above all the fact that our entrepreneurs at the moment have it too good at home to want to bother with foreign markets."

Thus, it appears that the very essence of the Moscow entrepreneurs, and particularly their efforts to maintain a privileged place by means of a totally artificial Chinese wall, are incompatible with the current tendency of Russian foreign policy and in fact go directly against it. It is clear that the most effective remedy for all Moscow's indolence and its trade practices, as well as for technological backwardness, would be Russia's transition to a liberal tariff policy, which would tear the Moscow district out of the hot-house atmosphere of monopoly and confront it with foreign competition in its own country. To us there is little doubt that the interests of absolutism in Asia on the one side, on the other the expansion of capitalist agriculture and the interests of the landowners, will sooner or later pull Russia down the road to a more moderate tariff policy. But, above all, a remedy can be created only in one way, namely by sharpening competition *within* the Russian customs borders, i.e., so that Moscow is ruthlessly abandoned to the unlimited competition of the progressive industrial districts of Poland and St. Petersburg. This viewpoint is also that which the more influential Russian press, such as the "Novoe Vremya," stressed explicitly in connection with the debate over the Czarist Empire's interests in Asia. That the government, for its part, is now in fact preparing to do away with Moscow's economic rut and to force the Muscovites toward modern production and trade methods is best proved by the most recent law on the maximum work day, which indicates the most abrupt break with Moscow's present methods of production, while it also appears as a realization of the *Polish* project of 1892.

To the same degree to which Moscow's economic conservatism is a drag on current Russian policy and becomes more so every day, Polish industry appears once more as Czarism's comrade in arms. We have shown by the comparison between the competitive conditions of Polish and central Russian production how far ahead of Moscow Poland is in terms of technology. For this reason alone, capitalist Poland, as the most progressive industrial district in Russia which, through competition, unceasingly spurs the others, particularly Moscow, toward technological improvements, realizes the Russian government's current program. But the Polish industrialists are also running ahead of the Russians specifically in the opening up of Asian markets. We have seen how seriously and thoroughly they prepared themselves for this task. Without awaiting the invitation of the government, they themselves seize the initiative and with their own hands forge trade links with foreign countries.

In the only country where Russian trade is relatively flourishing — in Persia — the products of the Polish textile industry make up nearly half of the total textile imports from Russia — approximately 40 per cent of the imports via the most important junction, Baku. To Poland also belong the initiatives toward trade relations with Persia, in many respects: already in 1887, thus before the government had turned its attention to this country, Poland had set about opening up its own trade agency and warehouse in Teheran. Lodz also immediately made use of the Trans-Caspian railway, to advance into Central Asia with its goods along with St. Petersburg and Moscow. It is the Warsaw district which provides the largely immigrant strata of the populations of Bukhara and Turkestan with glassware, faience, and porcelain, while the inferior Moscow products are bought by the poorer natives. Lodz is, at this point, the only industrial district in the Empire whose textile industry's products have found entry into Constantinople and the Balkan countries. Already in 1887, Poland had taken up trade relations with Rumania and Bulgaria. Recently Lodz began to send cotton products directly to Sofia. Indeed, the Polish bourgeoisie, through use of the Siberian railway line, may make Warsaw the center of the new, large European-Asian trade routes. "The British manufacturer," wrote the English consul in Warsaw, "may be prepared to find in them (the Polish entrepreneurs) formidable rivals in the markets of the East."

In this way Polish capitalism in Asia works directly into the hands of Czarist policy.

From these so diametrically opposed attitudes of Moscow and Poland toward the aims fixed by Russian policy, there also follows a totally different current in the public opinion of the two districts. Stronger and stronger grows the party favoring domestic free trade, favoring technological progress, the party which opposes the official guardianship and defense of backward industries, and therefore is sympathetic toward the Polish district; and the Moscow entrepreneurs stand more and more isolated with their ancestral belief in the Trinity: guarantees, bonuses, subsidies. The anti-Moscow temper clearly expressed itself on the occasion of Moscow's petition to the 1893 annual fair in Nizhni-Novgorod for the imposition of a tax on Polish traveling agents. Thus we read in *Novosti*: "During the same fair...these same representatives of protectionism composed and sent to the Finance Minister a petition regarding a special tax on the traveling salesmen of the Lodz factories, with the unconcealed intention of liberating the Moscow industrial district from Lodz's competition. According to healthy common sense, the Moscow manufacturers should, in the interests of Russian industry and of Russian consumers, merely follow the admirable example of the Lodz manufacturers and employ traveling salesmen, bring the producers closer to the consumers, and so cheapen and make easier the market for its own products. But not nearly so much entrepreneurial spirit lies with the customs and habits of these protection-coddled practical men; they prefer to try various pranks against their competitors." And, finally, a characteristic excerpt from the official government organ "Warsaw Tagesblatt" on the general tasks of Russia's industrial foreign policy: "With the opening up of these new markets in Central Asia and Persia, we reckon on the flourishing of our industries, and we repeat that it is very much to be deplored that the lion's share of the profits go to foreign countries, while only the crumbs remain for our poor workers (!). Our trade with Central Asia and Persia has not yet struck deep roots, and the representatives of Russian trade still have many victories to win over English competition to conquer those markets for Russia. *In view of the common enemy, the Moscow and Polish entrepreneurs should join forces in order to strive together toward the same goal...Russia's main goal in the Asian market is at this moment to exclude English goods. It would be a subsidiary question which of the Empire's industrial districts contributes more to the achievement of this goal,* if only the profits of industry on the banks of the Vistula went exclusively to the native population and not, as is the case, to increase the capital for German entrepreneurs, employees, and workers. Were those industries in the hands of *Russia or Poland*, then we would be far stronger in our battle with England, and our dominance in central Asia would be secured.''

Understandably, the government organ does not neglect to deal a blow in passing to the German industrialists, who are heavily represented in Polish industry; it charges them with ignoring Russian national interests, exclusive, egotistical concern for the ''German'' interests of their own pockets, etc. But in the main, we find here the actual situation of the moment, pointedly expressed: In view of the present tasks in the world market, the domestic rivalries of the Polish and Russian entrepreneurs stand completely in the background. Insofar as differences exist between them, the blame will be pushed onto the *Germans,* an element hated just as much by the Polish bourgeoisie, as we have seen. *Polish* industry in itself, its development, its flourishing, appear here in a new light, as lying directly in the interests of the Czarist government: Once it has served to additionally consolidate the Russian conquest in Poland, Czarism is now assigning Polish capitalism the flattering role of serving in Asia as the harbinger of Czarism's coming appetite for conquest. Indeed, Poland now plays the leading role, as we saw, in the realization of this lofty task, while Moscow's star, i.e., the special Muscovite economic policy, is slowly waning. The new Russian law on the maximum work day signifies that even in the Russian Empire the lovely days of Aranjuez — the days of primitive capitalist accumulation — are almost past.

Conclusion

Our task is finished. We believe that we can conclude from the foregoing that all apprehensions about the future of Polish industry—at least insofar as they relate to the danger threatened by the Russian government—are quite groundless and nothing but an uncritical, superficial reflection of the intimate entrepreneurial wrangle between the Lodz and Moscow entrepreneurs. If one looks deeper into the situation, one must arrive at the conclusion that Poland, in economic terms, not only does not have any separation from Russia in store, but, rather, the tendencies arising from the general internal nature of large-scale capitalist production itself are binding Poland much more strongly to Russia with every passing year. It is an immanent law of the capitalist method of production that it strives to materially bind together the most distant places, little by little, to make them economically dependent on each other, and eventually transform the entire world into one firmly joined productive mechanism. This tendency, of course, works most strongly within one and the same state, within the same political and tariff borders. The capitalist development of Poland and Russia has yielded this result. As long as both countries were predominantly agricultural and indeed natural-economy countries, thus until the 1860s, they remained economically foreign to each other and each represented for itself a closed whole with particular economic interests. Since factory production began here and there on a larger scale, however, since natural economy gave way to money economy, since industry became a determining factor in the social life of both countries, the self-containment of their material existence has more and more disappeared. Exchange and the division of labor has strung thousands of threads between Russia and Poland, and these manifold economic interests are so intertwined that the Polish and Russian economies today form more and more *one* complicated mechanism.

The process portrayed above is mirrored in many different ways in the consciousness of the different factors in Polish public life. The Russian government sees Poland as a tool for its plans for rule, believes that Poland has been unconditionally surrendered up to its power and that it has founded a thousand-year empire of despotism. The Polish bourgeoisie sees in this a fundamental of its own class rule in the country and an inexhaustibe source of riches; it indulges in the sweetest dreams of the future in its thoughts about Asia and believes itself able to build a thousand-year empire of capital. The various nationalist elements of Polish society perceive the entire social process as a unique, great national misfortune, which mercilessly shattered their hopes for the reconstruction of an independent Polish state. They sense instinctively the power of the economic bonds which capitalism has created between Poland and Russia, and, without being able to hold back the fatal process in reality, they can at least put an end to it in their own imagination; they cling in desperation to this illusion and expect the Russian government itself to nullify Poland's hated capitalist development with its own hands and so recreate a basis for nationalism.

We believe that the Russian government, the Polish bourgeoisie, and the Polish nationalists have all equally been struck with blindness, and that the capitalist fusion process between Poland and Russia also has an important dialectical side that they have completely overlooked. This process is bringing to fruition in its own womb the moment when the development of capitalism in Russia will be thrown into contradiction with the absolute form of government, and when Czarist rule will be brought down by its own works. Sooner or later, the hour will strike when the same Polish and Russian bourgeoisie which is today pampered by the Czarist government will become weary of their political attorney—Absolutism—and will checkmate the king. Moreover, this capitalist process is moving with impetuous haste toward the moment when the development of the productive forces in the Russian Empire becomes irreconcilable with the rule of capital and when, in the place of private commodity economy, a new social order based on planned, cooperative production will appear. The Polish and Russian bourgeoisies are hastening this moment with their combined forces; they cannot make one step forward without increasing and pushing forward the Polish and Russian working classes. The capitalist fusing of Poland and Russia is engendering as its end result that which has been overlooked to the same degree by the Russian government, the Polish bourgeoisie, and the Polish nationalists: the union of Polish and Russian proletariats as the future receiver in the bankruptcy of first the rule of Russian Czarism, and then the rule of Polish-Russian capital.

Appendix

A Note on Polish History

Poland's history during the first half of the nineteenth century, to which Rosa Luxemburg alludes in the early sections of her work, is tangled enough to warrant an explanatory note indicating its most important features.

The partition of Poland, the point at which Luxemburg begins her history of Poland's economic development, occurred in 1795 and was the third and final carving up of that country between Austria, Prussia, and Russia. Previously the Kingdom of Poland had represented a unique combination, economically backward yet, in certain respects, politically advanced. Although its economy was one of feudal agriculture based on serfdom, it was ruled through a parliamentary republic which elected the king and held a wide range of powers. The republic represented only the country's nobility, but this term embraced nearly a tenth of the population, ranging from the great landlords to impoverished freeholders.

THE INDUSTRIAL DEVELOPMENT OF POLAND

The 1795 partition erased Poland as such from the map, with the lion's share of the dismembered nation going to Russia. The nationalist fervor of the Polish nobility, the aspirations of the grindingly poor peasantry, and the reverberations that Poland's constitutionalist tradition found elsewhere in Europe were not so easily done away with.

In 1796, representatives of the nationalist Poles approached Napoleon with an offer to fight under his command in exchange for French support for Polish independence. The result was that Polish legions fought alongside the French in the Franco-Prussian War in 1806. Napoleon's debt to the Poles was not great enough, however, to convince him to undermine the entire continent's balance of power by forcing the resurrection of an independent Poland. Instead, the French leader and the Russian czar negotiated a "great power" agreement in 1807 that a portion of Prussia's Polish territories would be rechristened the Duchy of Warsaw, and placed under the rule of the king of Saxony, a neutral power leaning toward Napoleon. The Duchy included territories which had been under Prussian rule since the partition; after Napoleon's victories over Austria in 1809, it was expanded to include some of that empire's Polish territories as well. The Duchy's constitution, written in French, reflected Napoleon's influence: it established a near-absolute monarchy and a centralized state, and abolished serfdom, although largely only *de jure*.

Following Napoleon's defeat in the War of 1812, Russia invaded the Duchy of Warsaw and put an end to Napoleon's handiwork. Yet the 1795 partition's intention of permanently eliminating the Polish nation in any form was clearly no longer viable. At the 1814 Vienna Congress, the victorious powers—Russia, England, Austria and Prussia—reaffirmed the partition of Poland, but made permanent Russia's control of most of what had been the Duchy. It was now once again the Kingdom of Poland (thus the Congress Kingdom, or Congress Poland), with its own borders, passports, and constitution, but under the rule of the Russian Czar. The liberal constitution was modeled on that of the Duchy of Warsaw, but, in the hands of Russian absolutism, "theory and practice soon drew apart," in the words of one historian.

This was finalized in 1831, when an insurrection in Poland put

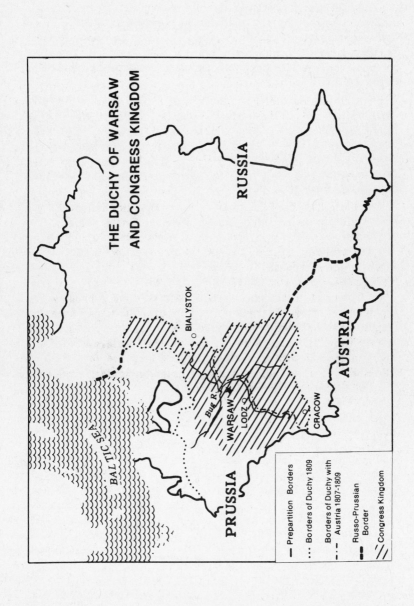

THE DUCHY OF WARSAW
AND CONGRESS KINGDOM

RUSSIA

BALTIC SEA

PRUSSIA

AUSTRIA

BIALYSTOK

Bug R.

WARSAW

LODZ

CRACOW

—— Prepartition Borders

···· Borders of Duchy 1809

—·— Borders of Duchy with
      Austria 1807-1809

━━ Russo-Prussian
      Border

/// Congress Kingdom

control of the country into the hands of rebellious nationalists for several months. As soon as Russia reestablished its control, the constitution of 1815 was suspended, and Congress Poland was firmly consolidated under Russian rule.

The volatile and unresolved peasant question and the dreams of the Polish nationalists continued to agitate Poland, however. The same unrest that had burst forth in 1831 flared fitfully in various parts of old Poland during the 1848 period. Following the Crimean War, an era of relaxation set in between Poland and Russia, highlighted by the 1856 announcement of reforms by the new czar, Alexander II, and the request three years later from the Russian government to the Polish Agricultural Society for proposals for large-scale land reform. In response came a crescendo of nationalist feeling in Poland, in tandem with a revolutionary wave that swept Russia. There were fights between crowds and police in Congress Poland, then demonstrations, building toward the Insurrection of 1863, which was definitively crushed by Russia only the following year.

In the aftermath, Congress Poland was reduced to a czarist province, and "russification" of Russia's Polish gubernias was undertaken more energetically than ever, together with the tightening of economic ties which Luxemburg describes. At the same time, the czar followed up his 1861 declaration freeing Russia's serfs with a complementary measure for Congress Poland in 1864, which finally consolidated the tentative steps out of feudalism begun under Napoleon's Duchy.

* * * * * *

Metric equivalents of Russian units of measure used in the text.

1 berkovez	= 163.80
1 pood	= 16.38 kilograms
1 Russian pound	= 409.51 grams
1 verst	= 1,066.78 meters
1 arshin	= 0.71118 meters
1 desyatin	= 1.0925 hectares

Bibliography

Constitution of the U.S. Labor Party, New York, 1976.

Deutscher, Isaac, *The Unfinished Revolution*, Oxford University Press, New York, 1967.

Engels, Friedrich, "Socialism: Utopian and Scientific," in Marx and Engels, *Selected Works*, International Publishers, 1968.

Ficino, Marsilio, "Five Questions Concerning the Mind," in *The Renaissance Philosophy of Man*, University of Chicago Press, Chicago, 1971.

LaRouche, Lyndon H., Jr., "Italy Lectures: What Only Communists Know," *The Campaigner*, December 1975.

—, "Rockefeller's Fascism with a Democratic Face," *The Campaigner*, November-December 1974.

(see also Lyn Marcus)

Lenin, V.I., *The Development of Capitalism in Russia*, Foreign Languages Publishing House, Moscow, 1956.

—, *The Right of Nations to Self-Determination*, Progress Publishers, Moscow, 1967.

Lukacs, Georg, "The Marxism of Rosa Luxemburg," in *History and Class Consciousness*, Merlin Press, London, 1968. Interesting as a reflection of how profoundly Rosa Luxemburg influenced the next generation of European socialists, and of how that influence was diluted and distorted by the subsequent campaign to purge the international movement of "Luxemburgism."

Luxemburg, Rosa, *The Accumulation of Capital*, Monthly Review Press, New York, 1951, 1968.

—, *Anti-Kritik, or What the Epigones Have Done to Marxian Theory*, in *The Campaigner*, New York, Winter 1971-Summer 1972. Luxemburg regarded this as her best work in economics, "an achievement...which will certainly outlive me." A rival English-language edition published in 1973 by Monthly Review Press, "balances Luxemburg's polemic with Bukharin's guttersnipe factional document from the thick of the anti-Luxemburg campaign."

—, *Briefe an Leo Jogiches*, Europäische Verlaganstalt, Frankfurt a.M., 1971. These letters offer a riveting insight into Luxemburg's early years and her development as a political leader.

—, *Einführung in die Nationalökonomie* (Introduction to National Economy). Only one section of this work has appeared in English translation, as the small pamphlet *What is Economics?*

—, *Gesammelte Werke*, especially Vol. I-1, Dietz Verlag, Berlin, 1972.

—, *The Mass Strike, the Political Party, and the Trade Unions*, Young Socialist Publications, Colombo, Ceylon (Bangladesh).

Marcus, Lyn (Lyndon H. LaRouche, Jr.), *Dialectical Economics*, D.C. Heath and Company, Lexington, Mass., 1975.

—, "In Defense of Rosa Luxemburg," *The Campaigner*, Spring 1973.

Marx, Karl, *The Civil War in France*, Foreign Languages Publishing House, Moscow.

—, and Friedrich Engels, "The Communist Manifesto," in *Selected Works*, International Publishers, New York, 1968.

—, *"Economic and Philosophical Manuscripts (1844),"* International Publishers, New York, 1964.

—, *The 18th Brumaire of Louis Napoleon*, International Publishers, New York, 1967.

—, and Friedrich Engels, *The German Ideology*, International Publishers, New York, 1939.

—, *Herr Vogt*, A. Petsch and Co., London, 1860. This pamphlet, which discusses European intelligence networks and their ties to terrorism, the press, and liberal circles, has yet to be published in English translation.

—, and Friedrich Engels, *The Holy Family*, Foreign Languages Publishing House, Moscow, 1956.

—, *The Poverty of Philosophy*, International Publishers, New York, 1963.

—, *The Secret Diplomatic History of the 18th Century and the Story of the Life of Lord Palmerston*, International Publishers, New York, 1969.

Nettl, J.P., *Rosa Luxemburg*, Volumes I and II, Oxford University Press, New York, 1966. The only biography of Luxemburg to step substantially beyond simple memorial tribute and discuss in detail her early years. Unfortunately, Nettl's staggering political incompetence (or is it deliberate?) makes his book useful only as a sourcebook, until a decent political biography is written.

Parpart, Uwe, "The Concept of the Transfinite," *The Campaigner*, January-February 1976.

"The Renaissance and the Idea of Progress," *The Campaigner*, January-February 1977.

Rose, Gerald, "The Social-Democracy's Roots," *The Campaigner*, March-April 1972.

Wandycz, Piotr S., *The Lands of Partitioned Poland, 1795-1918*, University of Washington Press, Seattle, 1974.

Wilson, Edmund, *To the Finland Station*, Doubleday and Company, Garden City, N.Y.

Index

Serfdom, 62, *93*, 179; abolition of, *84, 90, 94, 113, 120,* 180, 182; and forced labor, *84, 90*
Shaw, George Bernard, 29
Siberia, 75, *118, 167, 168, 171, 173*
Silesia, 33, *99, 105, 156*
SDKP, 66, 67, 68, 69, 70, 71
SDKPiL, 39, 52, 66, 66n
Socialism, 17, 36; factions within, 15, 16, 19, 29, 30, 34; scientific, 16, 17, 19, 20, 21, 26, 29, 30, 36, 46; utopian, 16, 17, 19, 22, 27, 28, 29, 30, 34-35, 37, 45, 45n, 46, 48, 51, 55
Socialist (Second) International, 65, 67, 68, 69, 70, 71
Social surplus, 21, 41, 42, 50
Sosnowiec, *107, 110, 126, 131, 151*
Soviet Union, 76
Sozialistische Monatshefte, 62
Spartakus, 61
Spinoza, Benedict, 19, 22, 23, 50
"Stages of national development," theory of, 52, 60, 61, 75
Steampower: use of in industry, *90, 100, 102, 121, 132, 139, 140, 141, 142*
Stirner, Max, 27, 28
Switzerland, 31, 64, 75

T

Tariff policy: effects on prices, *97-98;* of Russian Empire, *96, 97, 99, 100, 106, 110, 111, 112, 113, 120, 126, 144, 148, 149, 152, 153, 154, 155, 156, 157, 158, 159, 163, 168, 170, 172;* Russian-Finnish, *164;* Russian-Polish, *88, 89, 90, 93, 95, 105, 124, 125, 126, 127, 159, 162, 163*
Third National Bank (U.S.), 38
Tiplis, *118*
Transcaucasus, *118, 119, 127, 169*

Trotsky, Leon, 45, 45n, 61
Tsaritsyn, *118*
Tula, *131*
Turkey, 69, 70

U

Ukraine, 118
Usury, *84, 85, 120*

V

Van Buren, Martin, 38
Versailles Treaty, 17
Vienna Congress, *83, 88, 161, 180*
Vladivostok, *167, 168*
Volga region (of Russia), *127, 151, 152, 153*
Voluntarism, 43, 44, 49
Vorwärts, 68, 70

W

Wagner, Richard, 33
Warsaw, 62, *102, 103, 107, 111, 112, 119, 131, 150, 151, 153, 173, 174*
Warynski, Ludwik, 63
Webb, Sidney, 29
Weitling, William, 22
Weydemeyer, Joseph, 20, 20n
Whigs, 38
Workers Cause (Sprawa Robotnicza), 65, 66
Working Class, 21, 34, 35n, 35, 36, 42, 48, 52, 59, 60, 63, 65, *105, 165, 178*
World-historical, 26, 36

Z

Zero Growth, 28, 30, 38
Zinoviev, G., 45

Italicized numbers are references within Luxemburg's dissertation.